HOME FOR NOW

Making your rented space or first house beautiful

Joanna Thornhill

CICO BOOKS

LONDON NEW YORK

For Paul, for accompanying me through many decorating adventures in our successive home-for-nows

Published in 2014 by CICO Books
An imprint of Ryland Peters & Small
519 Broadway, 5th Floor, New York NY 10012
20–21 Jockey's Fields, London WC1R 4BW
www.rylandpeters.com

10 9 8 7 6 5 4 3 2 1

A CIP catalog record for this book is available from
the Library of Congress and the British Library.

ISBN: 978-1-78249-096-8

Printed in China

Editor: Alison Bolus
Designer: Vicky Rankin
Photographers: Emma Mitchell and James Gardiner
Stylist: Joanna Thornhill
Illustration: Harriet de Winton

CONTENTS

INTRODUCTION

In a matter of decades, property prices in many cities (and indeed, many countries) have spiraled beyond the means of many people. Where once the expectation was to rent for a period before making the short hop onto the property ladder, increasingly more of us find ourselves renting for years, or even decades, before taking what has now become a giant leap and purchasing a home. And with the rise in property prices, coupled with the colossal deposits often needed to secure that elusive first place, many new owners aren't exactly starting out in their dreamed-of "forever" home. Added to which, with precious little cash left to make changes to their new space, they may find they don't have the free rein they imagined they would, despite finally having the freedom to do what they want, unencumbered by a landlord's rules. While investing energy and resources into a temporary home might, understandably, not be a top priority, all but the shortest-term arrangements can seem rather lengthy when living in a space that is underwhelming or even disheartening to be in. However, these limitations needn't be boundaries to stop tenants and owners from transforming their house into a home.

Each property featured in this book demonstrates that rather than feeling burdened by the challenges of living in a place that can't really be changed (regardless of whether that's down to rules or financial restrictions), it is possible to be empowered by these circumstances. By embracing the inbuilt constraints, the people behind these homes (a fairly even mix of renters and home-for-now owners) have come up with some radical ways to transform their space into a vibrant home, with minimal outlay and a lot of imagination. Regardless of whether they view it as a short-term stop-gap home or a longer-term project, their attitudes to their homes are truly inspirational.

This book aims to illustrate the possibilities that can be achieved when taking a creative approach. From using a hanging rail as a room divider in an open-plan

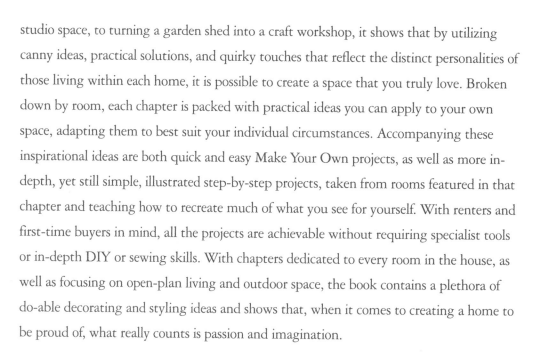

studio space, to turning a garden shed into a craft workshop, it shows that by utilizing canny ideas, practical solutions, and quirky touches that reflect the distinct personalities of those living within each home, it is possible to create a space that you truly love. Broken down by room, each chapter is packed with practical ideas you can apply to your own space, adapting them to best suit your individual circumstances. Accompanying these inspirational ideas are both quick and easy Make Your Own projects, as well as more in-depth, yet still simple, illustrated step-by-step projects, taken from rooms featured in that chapter and teaching how to recreate much of what you see for yourself. With renters and first-time buyers in mind, all the projects are achievable without requiring specialist tools or in-depth DIY or sewing skills. With chapters dedicated to every room in the house, as well as focusing on open-plan living and outdoor space, the book contains a plethora of do-able decorating and styling ideas and shows that, when it comes to creating a home to be proud of, what really counts is passion and imagination.

PREVIOUS PAGE Cheerful kitchen
A sunny yellow feature wall and fun accessories help to cheer up this basic kitchen.

OPPOSITE FAR LEFT Painterly display
Abstract canvases and interesting props help to add personality to a plain corner.

OPPOSITE LEFT Handy cubby
Don't disregard imperfect items—this unit's missing drawer makes space for a couple of books.

ABOVE Light and bright
Bold color can bring a tiny space to life, but temper with white to stop it feeling overpowering.

Notes for renters

• While your tenancy agreement may stipulate that you cannot make any changes to your home-for-now, if there is a specific task that you feel warrants doing, approach your landlord to discuss the possibility of doing it yourself, and see if you can find a compromise. They may have a no-painting clause, for example, but if one wall or room is in a particularly shabby state (or painted in a rather unfortunate color choice), try appealing to their good side by asking for permission to repaint it, to a professional standard, on the proviso that you will return it to its original color when your tenancy ends, if they so wish.

• Once you've built up a rapport, consider asking for a financial contribution for any works, or alternatively see if they would let you take a percentage off your next rental payment to cover some of the costs. While there are, of course, unscrupulous landlords out there, any decent landlord will appreciate a diligent tenant and recognize that attempts to make improvements to their property is mutually beneficial.

• If you plan on staying in the property for a while, use this as a bargaining tool and tell them how keen you are to make it feel like a home, and that you will feel far happier staying in the space for longer if you can make certain minor alterations. No landlord wants a property lying empty, and they may be more willing to budge if it makes for a happy long-term tenant.

• Always ask for permission before making any changes outside of the rules of your rental agreement, however minor. While you might not see how on earth your landlord could object to you removing their flea-ridden old shagpile carpet or painting over some dated patterned wallpaper, it is still part of their property, and you may find yourself in breach of the terms of your contract.

• Aside from aesthetic concerns, make sure your landlord carries out regular safety checks for gas and electrical systems and appliances (via professional organizations where appropriate), and ensure that any issues such as damp, security concerns, and access to heating and hot water are dealt with promptly, should they arise. Speak to your relevant local governing body, such as the Citizens Advice Bureau in the UK, if they will not cooperate with this.

Chapter One

LIVING SPACES

Even if yours is just a couple of old chairs and a makeshift coffee table in a corner, there's no reason why your SEATING AREAS shouldn't be comfortable and stylish. With WALLS AND DISPLAY playing a huge part in this, we've got lots of ideas for transforming your walls with both inexpensive and temporary decor. Clever STORAGE SOLUTIONS teach you how to make the most of what's available to you. Then finally, in OPEN-PLAN LIVING, we share ideas on both visually and practically separating areas of your space if you don't have the luxury of separate rooms.

Instead of a side table a storage cube with lift-off top provides a handy spot to store occasional items

Forget the rules about matching furniture sets and the notion of spending hours in soulless out-of-town furniture depots. When you're setting up a new home, be it your own or your landlord's, adopting a more fluid approach will allow you to create a far more interesting space, in a way that's flexible to your finances. And after fees and deposits, it's likely your funds will have taken a bit of a battering.

While it may take a while to get everything as you'd like it, creating a seating area, however modest to begin with, will give you somewhere to relax and entertain guests coming to visit your new place. Regardless of whether you already have furniture or it's a totally blank canvas, spend some time assessing your needs before making any purchases. What do you need to store in the room? How do you need to prioritize the accessibility of these items? Does the space need to double up with another use, such as a home office, or a guest bedroom when friends come to stay? If space is limited, make the most of every bit by running shelving right up to the ceiling, using every last scrap of space for storage (such as under and behind the sofa) and employing multifunctional furniture, like chests of drawers in place of sideboards, or a stool as a coffee table which can be used as additional seating when guests visit.

SEATING AREAS
Making living rooms cozy

BELOW Utilize a nook

An armchair and a small cabinet under a stairwell extends your living space right into the corners.

BELOW RIGHT Style your storage

If you need to use the space under the sofa for extra storage, keep things neat and chic in pretty vintage baskets.

OPPOSITE Mini side table

A small log, found on a walk, creates a cute mini table by a sofa without taking up much space.

Your seating will doubtless form a key element of your room, but chances are you may have to make do with less-than-ideal models at first. Loose throws are a great option here because they hide a multitude of sins, although they can look a bit messy. However, it's all in the styling: neatly tuck them over the sides and back for a more fitted look, or use fabric offcuts to create a valance hanging down from underneath the sofa cushions. Drape folded blankets over sofa and chair arms to disguise them and add a touch of color, with the bonus of having them to hand on chilly evenings.

In lieu of any shelving, make a statement out of a collection of coffee table books by stacking them on top of floor-standing cabinets

Wicker chairs sit just as well in the living room as in a sunroom or conservatory and can be a more lightweight, affordable alternative to armchairs

PREVIOUS PAGE Natural palette

Despite several design elements going on in this space, its predominantly nature-inspired color palette and motifs help to tie the look together.

BELOW Modern vintage

With an undeniable vintage vibe, this room still feels modern, thanks to contemporary textiles and quirky *objets*, such as this porcelain hand.

OPPOSITE A playful touch

The fun feel of this room isn't restricted to ornaments: here, a dividing wall is painstakingly yet inexpensively customized by wrapping it in children's plastic construction bricks. Its snug fit ensures it clings to the wall without any fixings, and can easily be removed if needed.

Embracing an eclectic look makes perfect sense in a home-for-now. Easy to add to and amend as you gather more pieces, this is a style that can be constructed very affordably. Forget preconceptions about what furniture should be used where, and utilize what you have got or what comes your way. For example, there's no reason why an old metal side table (perhaps more likely to be found as storage in the garage) shouldn't take pride of place beside the sofa. And if your table has no shelf underneath, make use of its storage potential anyway by piling high a collection of glossy magazines or books under it, tucking them out of the way. Items not intended as art, such as old measuring sticks, make decorative accessories in their own right. Keep your eyes peeled for similar interesting objects on your travels. The walls themselves can even be a key element in the space, such as the example on the right, clad in old scaffolding planks to add texture and warmth. Get the look in a less permanent way by cladding a large freestanding board in wooden planks, or use a *trompe l'oeil* woodprint wallpaper.

BELOW Flexible room plan

Moving furniture toward the center of a room, rather than lining it around its edges, can make for a more interesting layout. In smaller rooms like this one, this works best with lighter pieces, such as this loveseat.

OPPOSITE Alternative storage

Old suitcases and crates, such as those seen above and beside this wardrobe, provide plenty of living-room storage without detracting from the overall look of the room.

This flexible approach to furnishings allows you to make best use of what you may already have, with the benefit of providing a more informal, interesting look. A grand old wardrobe, no longer needed for clothes storage, can easily be converted into an armoire by installing simple shelves in its carcase. Alternatively, you could place budget freestanding bookshelves inside such a piece to get the look without doing any DIY. Likewise, a chest of drawers, usually confined to the bedroom, makes an excellent alternative to a sideboard or console table in an alcove, providing both display space and storage.

Decorative logs turn an empty fireplace into a feature

Curtains can make great room dividers, either in an open-plan space or simply in smaller rooms where there is no door

BELOW **Setting boundaries**
Placing a chair in the middle of the
room, like this one in the foreground,
visually defines the seating area in this
large multi-use room.

If you own your home or are renting an unfurnished apartment, chances are you
may not be able to afford to buy all of your furniture at once. Luckily, a mixture
of seating gives a far more contemporary look than the traditional three-piece
suite, as well as being a more affordable alternative. Focus on sourcing a main
sofa, then add chairs and armchairs as funds allow. Use whatever items are at
your disposal, such as an old crate as a coffee table, or a borrowed rug, while you
get yourself up and running.

Houseplants instantly add
a homey feel to any space.

NO SEW *Chair Upholstery*

No specialist sewing skills are needed to transform this surprisingly simple upholstered chair into a work of art.

1. Remove the chair pad and set aside. Sand all the wooden parts of the chair, then clean thoroughly with an old cloth soaked in white spirit. Leave to dry.

2. Brush the chair with the oil-based primer. Let dry.

3. Brush on as many coats of the high-gloss colored paint as you want until you are happy with the density of the color and the sheen. Try to avoid getting any paint on the fabric parts of the seat, although since these will be re-covered anyway, the odd spot doesn't matter.

4. Roughly cut out sections from your fabric and loosely pin them over the existing padded fabric sections on the arms, base, and back of the chair, taking into consideration where the fabric's pattern will sit. Using the existing padded sections of the chair as templates, mark their outlines onto your fabric with fabric chalk to create your new templates. Remove from the chair and cut out.

Renter's Alternatives

Painting might be out if you don't own the chair yourself, but you can still create a customized look. If you have some spare fabric and a free evening, give it a go:

- Fix the fabric on using safety pins rather than a staple gun, then use double-sided tape rather than glue to hold the fabric braid in place. Avoid doing this on anything of value in case of damage, and keep it to occasional rather than everyday chairs.

- Make a loose fitted cover for the whole chair, tucking your fabric into place as you go. Use a curtain tieback at the base of the seat, with the tassel hanging down the outside back of the chair, to act almost in the same way as a belt on a loose dress, giving it shape.

- Fabric (or a throw) needn't be the only option for covering your chair. Using an old, sturdy curtain could work just as well, or even some new canvas dustsheets (which you could dye to suit your room scheme), both of which can be sourced inexpensively.

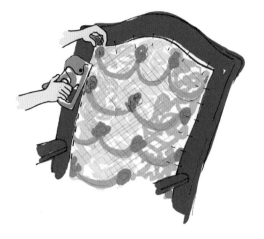

5. Iron the panel pieces and pin them in place, then go around each one with a staple gun, attaching the fabric along the edge of the existing fabric, and pulling it taut as you go. For the arms, add extra staples underneath where the two seams join up. Continue until all the parts of the chair are covered.

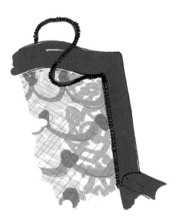

6. Using some fabric glue, secure the fabric braid around every fabric edge, making snips in the braid, as needed, to help maneuver it into position around any tight corners. Press the braid down securely, concealing all the staples, until the glue has dried.

7. Finally, cover the chair pad. If you're a keen sewer, you may want to sew a fitted cover with a gusset; if not, you can easily cheat by using some safety pins, as follows. Cut a rectangle of fabric approximately two and a half times longer than the pad; the width should be the width of the pad and sides plus 6 in (15 cm). Lay your fabric face down on a tabletop and place the chair pad on top, in the center. Fold the two longer lengths of fabric over the pad, one on top of the other, and pull taut, adding a line of safety pins along the top fabric edge to secure.

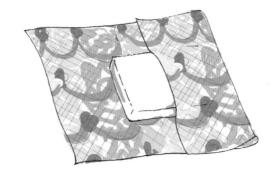

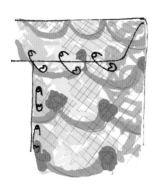

8. Take the first of the remaining short sides and fold it as if wrapping a present: taking the two corners and folding them in toward the chair pad. Lift the fabric up and over, keeping it taut, and fix it into place along the underside of the chair pad with another line of safety pins along the fabric's edge. Repeat on the other side. Once the fabric is secure, turn the chair pad the right way up and place back on the chair.

Handmade concrete letters, chosen as a mixture of significant initials and made in molds, are stuck direct to the wall using a hot glue gun

WALLS AND DISPLAY
Decorate your space

Whether you prefer streamlined, simple living or are an all-out maximalist, most of us would agree it's those finishing touches, like art on the walls and favorite homewares on display in pride of place, that make a house a home. But starting with a blank canvas can be somewhat daunting, especially if you're reluctant to paint or put holes in your walls due to rental agreements or the fear of making permanent alterations to your home-for-now. By following a few simple rules and employing some clever tricks, this needn't be the case.

From creating a gallery of artworks to displaying a prized collection of beach pebbles, all you need is a little creativity to curate your own exhibition-worthy displays and add that elusive homey touch. Walls themselves can take center stage too, regardless of how much decorating you are (or aren't) able to do. Think bigger than the ubiquitous feature wall and add some color and pattern, in some unexpected ways.

Small lightweight 3D decorations like these can be fixed to walls simply (and removably) with adhesive putty (Blu-Tack)

OPPOSITE Mix it up

Framed and loose items mix well alongside
a wooden animal head for an eclectic look.

BELOW A structured arrangement

Using a selection of smaller artworks, rather than
one larger piece, means you can use single nails
(or even removable picture-hanging strips) instead
of more heavy-duty fixings to hang, meaning less
(or no) damage to walls.

BELOW RIGHT Alternative art

Eschew frames to create a less formal arrangement
(and save money). Mount any larger designs onto
foamboard to give them a little more structure.

Creating a gallery wall, full of smaller artworks as well as
small 3D items, can be a less daunting and more cost-
effective process than investing in single, large pieces of art.
This approach allows you to build your display slowly over
time, as funds allow and your collection progresses. A bare
wall can be a daunting place to start, but be brave and fix up
your first central piece, then work your way outward from
there. Alternatively, lay out a mock-up on the floor before
you begin hanging. Keep everything quite closely packed,
with even spacing, to avoid the wall looking disparate and to
retain some structure. Place it in a central position above a
key piece of furniture, such as a sofa or sideboard. If in doubt,
try to keep a similar thread running throughout, such as color
or subject matter, though try to avoid being too formulaic.
Look beyond traditional photographs and prints and play
with ephemera, postcards, vintage advertising posters, and
even magazine cuttings for an eclectic, individual look.

MAKE YOUR OWN

Make the most of paint leftovers or tester pots and create your own inexpensive artwork with a cheap canvas. Dab on different colors with a small paintbrush to build up an abstract pattern, or draw on simple shapes such as squares or stripes. By using paints that also feature in the room where the canvas will be, you will help the scheme to tie together naturally.

Avoid the common mistake of hanging pictures too high. If in doubt, follow the guidelines art galleries use: hang any large artworks so that their center is 57—60 in (145—50 cm) from ground level, which is around the average human eye-height

RIGHT Colorful containers

Small cardboard gift boxes, glued together
to create a display space, make the perfect
spot to show off lightweight items. Line
each box with colorful paper offcuts for a
fun look, and attach them to the wall with
removable picture-hanging strips.

BELOW Printer's display

As well as holding an eclectic mix of
items, printer's trays can make a
feature of any repeat collections, such
as small shells from the beach or
decorative thimbles.

A step up from small 3D artworks, tiny ornaments and trinkets require
well thought-out, contained display storage in order to look considered
rather than cluttered. Vintage printer's trays are an excellent example
of this, and can be readily found at flea markets and online (see our
step-by-step guide to making something similar on page 43). Box
frames also make fetching displays, and can elevate items that are
relatively humdrum (a baby's first shoes, for example) into works of
art in their own right. For larger-scale displays, try mounting wine
crates onto your wall (or rest one on top of a cabinet) to house a mini
vignette of favorite ornaments.

Make a feature of favorite design books by displaying them on shallow picture ledges as an alternative to standard shelving

OPPOSITE Circles of color

The unusual skull print hiding this repro fireplace is balanced by the plain shield design above, whilst the pops of color in the paper garland add a quirky touch.

BELOW On reflection

A mirror is more commonly seen hanging above the fireplace, but positioned inside a recess it helps to reflect the room, improving the sense of space.

RIGHT Picture perfect

Avoid the temptation to mount a television on a chimneybreast. Instead, house it in an alcove, allowing a favorite artwork to take center stage.

Display opportunities run beyond your walls, however. A common casualty of unsympathetic renovations is the fireplace, and finding an original period beauty fully intact is becoming increasingly rare. But whatever you have inherited, there are ways to work with it. To disguise what's there, be it an ugly vent or a less-than-in-keeping modern fireplace, look out for decorative fireguards (vintage tapestry versions can often be found in second-hand shops), or simply lean a large artwork over it. Reinstate the area as a focal point by adding a shelf where an original mantelpiece might have been and display a collection of ornaments on top. Or if you've simply been left with an empty hole, view it as an additional styling opportunity and fill it with decorative items, candles, a fire basket dressed with logs, or even a disco ball to bounce light back around the room.

Adding wallpaper can seem somewhat daunting for the first-timer, and if you're renting, it's unlikely to be an option at all. But with a little thinking outside the box, there's no reason why patterned walls can't be a part of any home. If there's a paper you've fallen in love with, consider buying just one roll and suspend it as a single drop (try suspending it on a trouser hanger or wire hanger secured with clothes pins, or simply with a couple of small tacks at the top to take its weight). Alternatively, attach it to the front of a large sheet of wood using wallpaper paste or even spray adhesive, and lean this against your wall. Removable wall stickers, and, increasingly, removable murals and even wallpapers, have risen in popularity in recent years, and are perfect for commitment-phobes because they can simply be peeled off, leaving no trace when no longer required. Look beyond wallpaper, too, and consider alternative designs to adorn whole walls with: from book pages (see page 88 for a step-by-step guide) to the fronts of tea boxes, your imagination is the only limit.

If you're still not keen on sticking anything to your walls, consider paint instead. Forget the naff paint effects of the 1990s, however, and think about clever ways to add pattern: from painting on a simple stripe to creating a more decorative design, or even using a specialist patterned paint roller. When the time comes to neutralize it, simply paint back over to reverse the look.

Removable animal wall stickers add a fun twist to this stairwell

OPPOSITE Too good to recycle

Pretty packaging lives on in this clever stairwell (and is the perfect excuse to drink copious amounts of tea). Save up packaging from any favorite food to create a free feature wall (turn over to find out how).

BELOW Beauty in nature

Don't let artistic abilities (or lack thereof) put you off creating more intricate designs: here, photographs of twigs were projected onto a wall and the twig pattern simply filled in with white paint.

RIGHT Ways with wallpaper

Ask around your friends and contacts to see if anyone has spare offcuts of wallpaper that would be long enough for a single drop, or go halves with someone to save on costs if you don't need to buy a whole roll.

MAKE YOUR OWN

If you're up for doing something bold, really go for it: ask family and friends to contribute toward a postcard collection, for example, or go for a theme, such as floral vintage greeting cards or old cigarette cards. Then, when you have enough to cover a wall, simply stick down using adhesive putty (Blu-Tack) or sticky poster strips or, for a more permanent finish, try a glue gun or wallpaper paste (do a patch test first to make sure your chosen fixing method is strong enough). Cut to fit any awkward edges and overlap your designs for a patchwork effect.

LEFT **Ramp up the fun factor**

Anything goes in a jovial room like this: glasses tacked to a framed poster add a fun 3D touch, while the taxidermy and drinks tray sit resplendent on a vintage sideboard, providing stacks of storage.

BELOW Decorative door

As well as providing a spot to hang decorative accessories, this door could do double duty in the bedroom, by attaching a line of nails across it and using them to hang jewelry from.

Looking at wall coverings with a less literal approach can help you to see potential décor in a new light. While an entire wall covered in postcards creates an interesting backdrop as well as memory-inducing images, there are ways to get a similar feel on a smaller scale. Try simply introducing oversized decorative elements into a space, such as an old wooden screen, shutter, or door (this one was found in a skip). As well as providing an interesting backdrop in an otherwise plain white apartment, there is also the bonus of being able to hang decorative accessories, such as this handmade fabric wreath, directly to it rather than attaching them to walls. Old metal advertising signs and even antlers all add texture and personality. Allowing such pieces, along with larger artworks, to rest casually on the floor aids an informal feel, as well as avoiding damage to walls and surfaces.

ABOVE LEFT Colorful clip

A simple bulldog clip, spraypainted a vibrant color, is all you need for smaller artworks. For larger pieces, use one in each corner, to stop edges flapping and weigh down the bottom.

ABOVE MIDDLE Hang it up

String, twine, ribbon, or even fairy lights make a great line to hang postcards and photos from, securing them with miniature clothespins.

ABOVE RIGHT Push pin

Wood makes a forgiving surface to attach pictures to, so pop a thumbtack (drawing pin) through to hold small items in place.

LEFT Casually taped

Decorative masking tape (Washi tape) is excellent for hanging prints, as it is removable and yet can take a fair weight. Casually add some to corners of prints, or run it all around the edge of artworks to create a frame effect.

LEFT **New lease of life**

This is perfect for an old frame with missing glass: staple wire or fairy lights throughout the back of a bare frame, then suspend your artwork directly from this so that it appears to float in the center.

BELOW **Avoid drilling**

A picture ledge (or any existing ledge) provides a flexible home for prints—they can be easily swapped around or changed.

There's often a preconception that "grown-ups" should only display artwork in proper frames. But while rat-eared posters tacked to bedroom walls aren't exactly aspirational, there are plenty of creative alternatives to fixing up your art that don't involve either method. With imaginative display, the manner of fixing can be just as relevant as the print itself, turning disparate elements into a well-considered arrangement. Particularly in a home-for-now, or for people with an ever-changing collection, it may suit you to employ a system that allows for easy switching of artworks at a whim. For example, a grid of simple clipboards, arranged neatly on a wall, allows for regular chopping and changing of its contents, while a selection of embroidery hoops is a clever and lightweight way to display a collection of favorite fabric offcuts or vintage hankies.

RIGHT Colorful collection

Normally thrown away without a second thought, bottletops can be unexpectedly decorative in their own right, particularly when displayed *en masse* in a box frame.

Collecting can be a great and inexpensive (sometimes free!) hobby, with the benefit of injecting interest and personality into the areas where you showcase your finds. Often, it's not so much about what you collect as how you display it, and grouping the same items en masse makes a strong visual statement, whatever it may be. If you're looking to begin a collection, nature is a great starting point, so scour your local park or beach for interesting finds. For smaller items, curate your own miniature displays: a collection of beach-smoothed pebbles will look great stacked by size, whilst organizing buttons into multiple jars, arranged by color, is both practical and pretty. Arranging items in bowls, cake stands, or even clear glass vases keeps them contained without obstructing the view. As well as shelving, smaller collections are well suited to more compact areas, such as along a picture ledge or windowsill.

Mixing collectibles alongside everyday items stops things feeling contrived, and allows you easily to allocate more or less space for things as your possessions fluctuate. And if your collections are practical pieces in themselves, display them to their best advantage while still keeping them accessible. A large collection of mismatched colored crockery deserves to be seen and would look wonderful arranged in color-blocked stacks on some open shelves, for example, or use a collection of tea caddies to store different types of your favorite brews.

An old fireplace hole makes an ingenious cocktail bar within a kitchen, with a glass shelf added for extra storage

RIGHT Tailored shelving
Basic MDF shelving provides
invaluable storage in an otherwise
redundant space, cleverly following
the curve of the stairs.

**BELOW LEFT Champagne-top
treasures**
Even litter can be display-worthy
when viewed with fresh eyes, such as
these discarded Champagne tops
twisted into whimsical miniature seats.

**BELOW MIDDLE & RIGHT
Beachcombing bounty**
Unified by its muted colors and
natural shapes, nature often provides
wonderful display material.

LEFT Unusual arrangement

Vases needn't store just flowers. This one is used for a clever display of animal skulls—an unexpected way of showing a macabre collection.

ABOVE LEFT Trinket tray

Grouping ornaments together on a tray can make a stronger statement than spreading them out, and is more practical for cleaning, too. An inexpensive display of vintage glass and spraypainted bottles, a favorite candle, and an old shoe last are brought to life with inexpensive Gypsophila and a chrysanthemum.

ABOVE Books suspended

This repurposed press makes for an innovative bookshelf, keeping favorite tomes close to hand.

VINTAGE DRAWER *Display Shelves*

If display space in your home is non-existent, but you can't drill shelves into your walls, then an old drawer and some stripwood could be just the answer to your decorative dilemma. By using any leftover paint and strips of wood you might have at home, this freestanding display case could cost very little to produce. DIY-phobes needn't be put off, because no drilling or specialist tools are required for the job, just a little sawing and a steady hand.

You Will Need:

Old wooden drawer (check with friends and neighbors if they have any spare, or look in skips, or ask an employee at your local dump to put one aside for you)

White spirit

Old cloth

Tape measure

Pencil

Tester paint pot or some leftover paint—wood paint or standard emulsion

Paintbrush

Length of thin pine stripwood that's narrower than the inside of your drawer, and long enough to provide as many shelves as you require

Second length of thin pine stripwood, ³/₄ in (2 cm) narrower than the first, and long enough to provide as many upright shelf dividers as you require

Third length of thin pine stripwood, around ³/₄–1 in (2–3 cm) wide and long enough to divide into two battens for each shelf

Clamp

Hacksaw or wood saw

Sandpaper

Spirit level

Wood glue

1. Clean your drawer thoroughly using some white spirit and an old cloth.

2. Work out how many internal shelves you want, and at what heights, using a tape measure, then mark these points inside the drawer with a pencil.

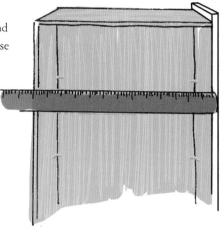

3. Paint the widest and second-widest lengths of stripwood in a color of your choice and leave to dry. Apply a second coat, if required.

4. Once the painted stripwood is dry, take the wider piece, which will form your shelves, and mark with a pencil the cuts you need to make to create each shelf. It is vital that you cut them to the exact width of the inside of the drawer to ensure a snug fit. Clamp the wood to a workbench or table, then carefully saw along each line. Sand the ends to remove any rough edges.

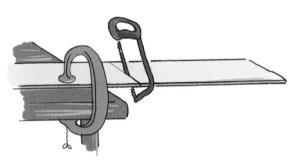

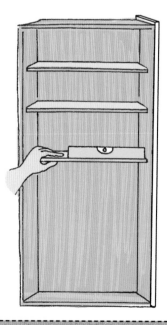

5. Slide each shelf into position within the drawer—you want to aim for a snug fit but without causing the drawer to bow. If any shelves are too wide, sand the edges further until they slot into place. Stand the drawer upright on a flat surface and, using a spirit level, gently nudge each shelf slightly, as necessary, until it is flat and level, supporting it underneath with your hand.

6. Once all the shelves are in place, lay the drawer down flat and prepare the support battens by sawing the narrowest length of stripwood so that it provides two battens per shelf, each roughly ¾ in (2 cm) shorter than the depth of your shelves. Sand all the ends, then add a small strip of wood glue to the first batten and stick it into position underneath the shelf edge, on the inner side of the drawer. Hold in position for a minute until the glue has set, then work your way around the drawer until each shelf has a batten at both ends. Wipe away any excess glue with a damp cloth before it dries.

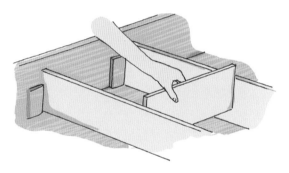

7. Once all the battens are dry, decide where you want the upright shelf dividers to fit. These are purely decorative rather than functional, so you may like to plan them to accommodate any specific ornaments you wish to display. Measure the exact height between each set of shelves you wish to place one in, then saw off the required lengths and sand each end. Slot into position, sanding further if the fit is too tight, until each riser fits comfortably into position without the need for any further support to hold it in place.

Make the most of deep shelving by pushing books toward the back to provide extra storage space in front

Spiraling property prices and rental charges mean that increasingly we are living in smaller and smaller homes, so it goes without saying that most of us are pushed for storage. And in a home-for-now, the problem can be trickier still, as spending thousands on bespoke fitted storage is unlikely to be an option. But with clever planning and savvy shopping, it's possible to marry the aesthetic and the practical in one happy union.

It's no coincidence that the trend for painted furniture coincided with the last big recession: think of it as your interiors secret weapon, ready to turn even the most dated and dull furniture into something far more appealing, rather than simply hitting the shops for something new. Before throwing anything away, or rejecting offers of hand-me-downs, look at everything with fresh eyes—if it still serves its function, simply change its look. And if it doesn't do that, can you repurpose it? Adding wicker storage boxes onto a shelving unit could instantly turn it into a handy piece for the bathroom to store towels and toiletries, while converting a redundant wardrobe into an armoire could be as simple as screwing in some shelves (seen opposite). Likewise, it could function as something else, such as an old sideboard as a TV cabinet, with games consoles and DVDs tucked away inside. If you can't make permanent changes to furniture because you don't own it, play with fabrics where you can, or experiment with wall stickers or contact paper/sticky-backed plastic (after doing a patch test) for an instant transformation.

STORAGE SOLUTIONS
Clever ways to control the clutter

Building site bounty

Old scaffolding planks make sturdy (and sometimes free!) shelves. Cut each length to size and support on wooden battens at either end. Ask a local scaffolding firm if they have any old, decommissioned boards going spare.

OPPOSITE Made to measure

This built-in narrow shelving, designed with paperbacks in mind and constructed cheaply from simple wooden battens, runs floor to ceiling, despite the sofa covering its lower half (which makes this section ideal for storing lesser-used items that don't require constant access).

Suggesting the use of shelves to store your books, magazines, or music collection is nothing new. But think carefully before buying or installing anything, as clever planning will stand you in good stead. Consider what it is you wish to store, and what would best suit this need. For example, if your book collection consists almost solely of paperbacks, then tall, deep shelving might not be the best use of space. And if you regularly add to your collection without purging any old tomes, you will soon run out of space if you only plan for what you currently have. If fixing shelves to the wall is an option, explore this route: it's often the best way to get exactly what you need and can be much cheaper than buying freestanding units if you install it yourself. But if freestanding is your preference, it's wise to source pieces that can be added to and amended as your storage needs change.

RIGHT Surprising stackable storage

These clever shelves are actually several single-height units stacked together to make a bespoke record tower.

Adding castors to a bookcase can be useful in a multipurpose living space, allowing you to alter the layout easily

FAR LEFT AND LEFT
Use chairs

When not otherwise engaged, a spare chair looks resplendent dressed with display pieces, such as a stack of pretty vintage books or a pitcher of flowers.

OPPOSITE **Seat by the sofa**

In a small space, a side table might not be viable, so use a chair instead for both temporary surface space and guest seating when required.

RIGHT **Stool with books**

Tucked away in a corner, an old stool provides a great additional space to store coffee table books, both perched on top and balanced between its legs, and is easy to clear for additional seating, if required.

Often, when you're strapped for space and cash, the furniture you do have has to multitask, and the humble chair is no exception. Unless your sitting room is exceptionally well equipped, it pays to have a few spare chairs around the place for those times when one guest too many comes by, but for the times when it's just you and your household, put them to good use in other ways: as handy spots for storage and display. Use them for both purposes, while ensuring they are easy to clear when needed again for their intended function. A step stool may well be a useful investment, or even a footstool or pouffe for more casual seating, which can also double as a coffee table if topped with a tray. Unlike matching sets, odd chairs can often be sourced for very little money or even found by the roadside. If you're not so keen on the mismatched look, paint all your chairs the same color to minimize the differences between them.

Add interest to old metal candlesticks and candle holders with some enamel paint; play with matte and gloss to vary the finish

MAKE YOUR OWN

Jazz up an old piece of furniture and add a twist to a classic lace print with this easy-to-replicate design. Paint the furniture (using a paint appropriate for its material, and priming it first if necessary), then lay an old lace tablecloth or curtain over the top, taping it taut and into position. Take it outside, then coat with a couple of layers of vibrant spraypaint and let dry; then remove the lace.

OPPOSITE Dressed in lace
Arrange the contents of a partially exposed unit so that the less-lovely items are hidden, with the more appealing ones out on show.

Adding bold color to furniture is a great alternative to adding it to your walls, and it can be either a temporary or permanent affair, depending on whether you own the piece or not. As seen opposite, lace and bold colors combine to give a surprisingly modern look. To keep clutter out of sight on an open console unit, simply drape a piece of lace (or any other fabric) over the top to act as a partial disguise. Alternatively, or for something a little more permanent, see above.

ABOVE LEFT Fun display

Teenaged boys' rooms are notoriously difficult to decorate. Vintage crates work well to display the quirky belongings of this resident youngster.

ABOVE Flip it over

Using an upturned crate as an impromptu coffee table creates a casual air, as well as offering a storage cubby beneath it.

LEFT Handy store

Make a feature out of firewood by storing it in a stack of reclaimed wine crates. Adding castors to the bottom makes the set-up easier to move if required. Introducing an industrial touch, this unusual lamp was created using an old tripod as its base.

You don't always have to use bona fide furniture in every room. In fact, making do with what you can get your hands on is often part and parcel of the home-for-now approach. Sturdy old wine or apple crates have multiple uses, and they feature throughout the book as characterful alternatives to shelves, cupboards, and even tables. Mount several in a line along a wall, or stack them on top of one another to form a freestyle shelving unit. Keep them as they are for a rustic look, or line their backs with posterboard (cardboard) and cover with plain or patterned paper, to add a contemporary twist. Smaller fruit crates, often freely available at fruit and veg markets, are good for smaller items, and can also be used under sofas or inside cupboards to help keep things organized (see page 102 for a great step-by-step fruit-crate project). Suitcases, too, make a great makeshift table: stack a few together for height to act as a side, coffee, or even night table (bedside table). If they're looking a bit scruffy, give them a blitz with some spraypaint to transform them into a "matching" set.

(see page 102 for a great step-by-step fruit-crate project)

BELOW
Pack up your suitcase
An old suitcase creates a novel basis for this temporary DJ station, with space to store lesser-played records inside it.

Even the tiniest of spaces can still contain a makeshift hallway storage area. If you have the space, a freestanding wardrobe could be a canny take on built-in cupboards, especially if tucked away in a corner. Or for a more flexible (and smaller) alternative, try a smart clothes rail or even a vintage-style locker unit. Don't forget to utilize the back of the door, too, either with drilled-in hooks or an over-the-door set.

ABOVE Storage on display

In a studio space where everything's out on show, try to make storage a part of the décor rather than a disguise. Vintage suitcases look classy out on show and provide useful storage for non-essential hallway items, such as winter knits and occasional shoes (then when you're going on holiday, simply empty them out!)

RIGHT Multitasking bench

Stretching an extra-wide coat rack across a hallway is a wise use of space if you have no separate cupboard space for coats. A long bench offers a comfortable place to perch, and the area beneath it can be used to tuck shoes away neatly.

Chest of Drawers Makeover

When adding pattern to your walls isn't an option, try adding it to your furniture instead.

1. Remove all the drawers from the chest and stand them, and the carcase itself, in a well-ventilated space.

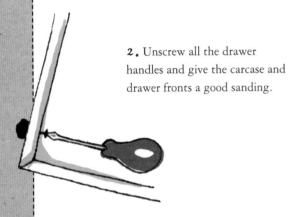

2. Unscrew all the drawer handles and give the carcase and drawer fronts a good sanding.

3. Brush off all the sawdust, then wipe the carcase and drawers clean using a cloth and white spirit. Let dry. Meanwhile, unroll the wallpaper, turn it over and then roll it up again gently to flatten it.

4. Paint the carcase in your chosen color. If the carcase is solid wood, paint it first with some oil-based primer, then paint it with either eggshell or gloss paint, depending on whether you want a matte or shiny finish. If the carcase is melamine or veneer, you will need to use a specialist melamine primer, or you could try a chalk-based paint, which will adhere to the surface without the need for any primer. Apply a second coat if required.

You Will Need:

An old chest of drawers

Screwdriver

Sandpaper: fine, medium, or coarse, depending on the condition of the chest

Old cloth

White spirit

Wallpaper off-cuts, large enough to cover the drawer fronts

Primer, if required (see step 4 for guidance)

Paintbrush

Paint in a color that either ties in with or contrasts with your chosen wallpaper

Pencil, ruler, and eraser

Scissors or craft knife

Foam brush

Strong white craft glue, diluted if necessary (see step 8)

Credit card

Thin skewer

Electric drill (optional)

New handles (optional)

Renter's Alternatives

If your landlord owns your furniture as well as your walls, you can still add color without risking your deposit.

- Use the same technique of sticking wallpaper to drawer fronts, but instead of glue, use double-sided tape around the edges to secure the paper. This should clean off easily from modern melamine items, but it's best to do a patch test in a corner first to make sure. This technique is best avoided on antique pieces.

- Decorate the front with removable wall stickers or strips of decorative masking tape (Washi tape), using a craft knife to break the run over each drawer front.

- Add some interest to a plain chest by adding pretty new handles, keeping the existing ones somewhere safe ready for swapping back when you move out.

5. Lay the wallpaper pattern-side up on a table. Place your first drawer front face down on top of this, positioning it where you want its pattern to fit on the drawer front. If your drawers are wider than the wallpaper, you may prefer to place the drawer lengthwise on the paper, to avoid needing to use two lengths joined together on the front. Lightly draw around the edges of the drawer front to create a faint outline.

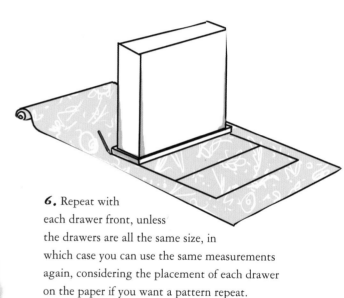

6. Repeat with each drawer front, unless the drawers are all the same size, in which case you can use the same measurements again, considering the placement of each drawer on the paper if you want a pattern repeat.

7. Trim off the paper from the remainder of the roll with scissors or a craft knife and ruler. Cut out each paper drawer front using sharp scissors or a craft knife and ruler. If any pencil lines are still visible, rub these out.

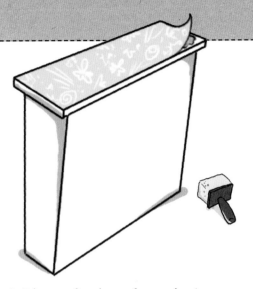

8. Take your first drawer front and, using a foam brush, coat it with a thin layer of craft glue. If your chosen glue is thick, dilute it with a little water until it is easy to spread. Pay special attention to the edges and corners. Position the wallpaper in place, carefully pushing out any bubbles with a credit card to ensure a smooth result. Wipe off any excess glue—don't worry if it looks unsightly as it will dry clear. Leave the paper to dry and repeat with the other drawers.

9. Cut off any excess paper protruding from the drawer edges using a craft knife. For extra durability, apply another thin layer of craft glue to each drawer front with a foam brush, and leave to dry.

10. Use a thin skewer to help you locate the original screw holes in each drawer front, then screw the handles back on. Alternatively, if you wish to use a different type of handle, make some new holes first, using an electric drill.

An ugly storage heater is cleverly disguised during summer months with this handmade fabric cover

The term "open-plan" is often bandied about in architectural design magazines to describe grand, cathedral-esque loft spaces. But for most of us, the reality of open-plan living is closer to a modest room that has several different functions shoehorned into it. With creative planning, though, there's no reason why even the most bijou of abodes can't still enjoy separate living "zones" along the same sort of lines, albeit on a somewhat smaller scale.

This tiny one-room studio apartment (opposite) would, on paper, sound like a recipe for disaster. It is the sole residence of a freelance designer who also works from home and has a penchant for collecting vintage fabrics and trinkets, with a love of bright color and pattern. But by creating the space with conviction, whilst utilizing every last nook and cranny, the result is a cheery, colorful, and (most importantly) uncluttered space, where every last detail is carefully considered without having to make aesthetic compromises. Far from feeling overpowering, the bright tones, kept to a limited palette, help to unify the space and create pockets of interest throughout it, meaning that as the eye flits around, the room feels rich and full.

OPEN-PLAN LIVING
Working without boundaries

Where possible, breaking up an open-plan room with furniture often makes for a more interesting and user-friendly space. Here, the sofa resides well away from any walls, creating a hallway-style space behind it and providing a more intimate feel, despite being part of a larger space (see below and opposite). Placing an old farmhouse-style table in such an industrial setting looks anything but twee, and every available bit of surface space, from the deep window ledges to the tops of kitchen cupboards, is utilized for displaying an interesting collection of art and *objets*. Splashes of color, from the vibrant yellow kitchen feature wall and accessories throughout, help to add interest to the space but are tempered by the expanse of clean white walls.

OPPOSITE A vibrant mix

Although there is a lot going on in this small space, the mixture of styles and colors of furnishings actually helps to create a look that is united by its lack of rigid formality.

BELOW Wall of shelving

A bank of inexpensive low shelving units makes for seamless, unobtrusive storage along this wall, giving a built-in look and stopping at just the right height to provide display space on its top.

Old linen tablecloths make great no-sew curtains: attach them to an existing curtain pole with wire clips or fabric ties made from ribbon

MAKE YOUR OWN

A runner instantly smartens up a tabletop without feeling as formal as a full tablecloth. It's also a great use for scraps or offcuts of fabric, particularly if your table is small. Measure out some fabric and cut it to around half the width of your tabletop, and around 20 in (50 cm) longer. Place it right-side down on an ironing board with one short edge resting on the board, then take some iron-on hemming tape and lay it on top of the fabric's wrong side, about 1 in (2.5 cm) from the edge. Turn the fabric up to cover the tape, then run over it with a hot iron to seal the hem in place. Repeat on the other short end, then on each long side.

To help blur the lines between a cooking and living space, open shelving in the kitchen can really soften the boundaries. But rather than ripping down cupboards, try simply removing the doors for an instant (and reversible) transformation. By using decorative items in the space, such as plants, ornaments, and even lamps, the union feels even closer. Make the most of any gaps between cupboards by installing hanging bars for pots, pans, and plates, and keep any key design elements, such as fresh green floral touches, on show throughout the space for consistency.

ABOVE Divide your space

A storage bench helps visually divide the kitchen and living space in this open-plan room, as well as providing additional seating for the dining table.

OPPOSITE Color blending

Strips of colored masking (Washi) tape add fun, removable color to the edges of these kitchen cupboards, and tie in with tones used in other parts of the room.

Tacking a pretty tablecloth over a freestanding washing machine helps blend it into the space

An oversized teacup planter makes a welcome change from a vase of flowers (and will stay in bloom for much longer, too)

Vintage elements in the room, such as
the wood walls and leather sofa, are
brought into the twenty-first century
thanks to contemporary accessories—
note the modern chevron cushions
and fun art.

BELOW **Kitchen brights**
A monochrome structure means that bright and
colorful accessories pop right out of this kitchen
setting. Cupboard tops make a handy spot to store
cookery books.

It's often harder to add character into a new-
build apartment than an older property.
Without period features or charming quirks,
such a blank canvas can easily feel devoid of
personality. This space is a textbook example
of how to buck that trend, however. The
wood-clad walls instantly add warmth and
personality, and are complemented with an
array of crisp, modern art prints.

The curves of this round dining table,
placed between the kitchen and living room to
create a natural barrier between the two, helps
the flow of the room, and can be extended
when extra guests visit. A cheap vintage
internet find, it is paired with new designer-
inspired chairs: another online bargain.

Many newbuilds come with a standard
white gloss kitchen that, while perfectly fine
and neutral, can feel somewhat dull, especially
in a space like this, which is otherwise
brimming with individuality. As replacing
new fittings and fixtures purely for aesthetics
is both costly and wasteful, here humorous
touches were added to marry in elements from
the rest of the space. Removable wall stickers
in this quirky moth design run across the
cabinets, picking up on the slightly macabre
touches seen elsewhere in the room, and a
splashback painted in chalkboard paint allows
for drawings and notes to be jotted onto it as
an ever-changing design element.

BELOW Dreamy daybed
A daybed provides a chic (and often cheaper) alternative to a sofabed, without compromising on style, which is perfect when your living space has to double as a guest room.

OPPOSITE Mix and match
Sourcing dining chairs separately from the table, rather than splashing out on a whole matching set, feels more modern and is often a less costly approach, too.

Of course, if color and quirk isn't your thing, then a predominantly neutral look doesn't have to mean boring, and a pale, limited palette will aid a calm, soothing atmosphere. Add interest with textures, as seen here in the mixture of natural and painted wooden furniture, vintage linen covering the storage chest (which doubles as a coffee table), and the slightly industrial-looking chairs (actually designed for outdoor use, so as such can be easily taken outside for summer al fresco dining). Wrought iron is a classic material, and is great for small spaces because its delicate uprights visually take up less space than solid furniture pieces, which all helps with the open feel of the space. Using furniture to divide a multifunctional room is an easy way of creating distinct zones. Here, this has been achieved without being oppressive by using a glass-fronted cabinet that isn't too high, allowing light to bounce around the room. Pretty dining accessories, such as favorite teacups and cake stands, make for an attractive as well as functional display.

Dated window pelmets, which the tenant is not able to remove, have been cleverly disguised by pinning a minimal gray linen fabric over them

Chapter Two

KITCHENS AND DINING

Often considered the heart of the home, the KITCHEN can be a particular challenge in a home-for-now and for renters, it's unlikely that you can make any big changes here at all. However, even if you do own, the chances are that you aren't able to (and wouldn't wish to) spend a fortune creating your ideal dream space when you may not be in it for all that long. As social needs change, the DINING SPACE is increasingly becoming part of the kitchen area, too, which leads to a demand for a more social and multi-purpose room. In this chapter, kitchen and dining areas are uniquely tailored to reflect the personalities of each resident, whether they own or not, creating stunning spaces that go far beyond the functional.

IT PAYS TO

BUY GOOD TEA

Fix the lids of herb and spice
jars to the underside of your
wall cabinets, using wood glue or
removable picture hanging strips,
to free up your countertop

KITCHENS

Painting, primping, and personalizing

It's easy to think in fairly black-and-white terms when it comes to kitchens: you either put in a new one, or you put up with the old one. What the kitchens in this section show, however, is that there are various shades of gray in between and much that you can do with a little imagination, whatever your circumstances. Practical considerations must take precedence, of course. Do you have enough cabinet storage for foods, crockery, and bakeware? If you're a keen cook, do you require space for herbs, sauces, and spices to be close at hand? Where are you going to hang dish towels and aprons? From the aesthetic, such as hiding and disguising elements with paints, fabric, and new surfaces, to practical ideas, like retro-fitting units with shelf inserts and handy boxes to make better use of existing cabinets, there is much that can be done to improve any space without undertaking major work.

This cool mid-century space, opposite, employs many clever ideas to help personalize it. An ex-public apartment (council flat), its 1960s origins aren't hard to make out. Mismatched reclaimed wood clads the units (copy the look by having panels cut to size and attaching them to existing cabinets with wood glue), while the countertop is actually covered with bamboo floorboards, for an eco-friendly, hardwearing, and unusual surface. The window treatment has been given a twist, too, with some favorite vintage fabric transformed into a practical roller shade (blind) using an inexpensive online kit. What unites this space, and the others featured, is that rather than feeling like a separate part of the home, the decorative and clever touches used within them integrate perfectly with the rest of their space.

OPPOSITE Pale and interesting

Despite at first glance looking like a fully fitted kitchen, the drawer unit next to the stove is actually totally separate, yet is painted to blend in with the rest of the units and topped with an offcut of worktop to complete the tie-in.

RIGHT Practical metal buffet

Originally used to store lab equipment, a metal cabinet is practical in a kitchen and can be kept clean with a quick wipe. Pretty vintage crockery stored inside avoids looking too girlie, thanks to its industrial note.

BELOW Fill the gap

Rented kitchens can often have odd gaps under countertops, left from long-discarded appliances. Here, a vintage bookcase fits the spot perfectly and becomes a stylish, useful place for crockery, kitchenware, and cutlery (stored in a bowl).

Fitted kitchens are very much the norm these days, although freestanding designs are rising in popularity, thanks to the flexibility they offer. Freestanding furniture can supplement your storage in a kitchen space, and helps to loosen the formality of the room, too. However small the gap, there's usually something to be found to fit it—and it needn't be a purpose-built kitchen item. An old bookcase, piece of office furniture, or even a chest of drawers can work perfectly well. Keep practicality in mind, and ensure that your chosen pieces can withstand the uses you assign to them. For example, a lacquered wooden tabletop may not handle multiple food spills well, whereas a metal cage locker might make a great corner pantry. Keep an eye out on vintage shopping trips for freestanding kitchen units from the 1940s and 50s. Kitchens often comprised unfitted pieces during this time, and as well as being specifically designed for the job, they often look charming, too, even if they are hidden under years of grime or a bad paint job. To create a unified look, choose pieces that are similar in style to your existing units, or coat everything with the same paint to diminish the differences. Alternatively, if eclectic is more your thing, embrace the contrast between each element.

Lesser-used items, such as cake tins and cooking pots, can add personality to a neutral kitchen as well as making use of redundant storage space

RIGHT Add some greenery

Plants can help to soften the look of any space.
A high corner shelf, which isn't easily accessible
for storage, utilizes the nook in a useful way.
Choose a plant that doesn't require daily
watering if the spot is hard to reach.

BELOW Decadent detail

There's no reason why wallpaper can't be used
in certain areas of a kitchen, but to protect it
from splashes, you could brush on a coat of clear
decorator's varnish to create an easy-wipe finish.

Open shelving is a great way to make a feature of favorite crockery,
bakeware, and even food packaging, and can be far more cost-effective
than fitting additional cabinets. A basic shelving system, with metal
uprights and repositionable brackets, is a perfect no-frills foil for a pretty
kitchen collection, and gives you the flexibility to alter shelf heights with
ease to accommodate possessions as your needs change.

An even simpler way to get the look, as touched on in the previous
chapter, is simply to remove cabinet doors to create some instant open-
plan shelving. Breaking down some of the formality of a room, these
open cabinets also provide an extra spot to style vignettes of favorite
crockery or kitchen supplies that would otherwise go unseen. Consider
blending the open units in with the remainder of your décor by painting,
or even wallpapering, the cabinet backs (fixed with double-sided tape if
you may need to reverse the look). Alternatively, to enjoy the best of
both worlds, remove just some of the doors, enabling you to keep the
nicest bits on show and the rest hidden away.

ABOVE Light the way

Boost the task lighting in your kitchen, as well as highlighting a display area, by attaching a clamp light to some open shelving.

LEFT A flexible option

Adjustable shelving of this type can be a great solution for rentals. If your landlord is reluctant to put up shelving for you, see if you'll be allowed to install a similar system on the basis that it can be customized to suit future tenants.

ABOVE Crate kitchenette

Create a handy storage space for everyday crockery and baking items on your countertop by using a simple fruit crate. Add some cup hooks inside it and keep the top free for displaying extra items, or simply build up the height with additional crates.

ABOVE RIGHT Sugars and sprinkles

Nothing feels quite as much fun in the kitchen as a display of cake sprinkles, decanted into jars and ready for use every time there's an occasion to bake for. Both the shelf edges and jar lids have been customized using decorative masking tape.

RIGHT Spices on show

Placing an old drink bottle crate on its side creates a novel standing perch for storing herb jars. Decanting them into mini glass jars and labeling them with a label-maker adds a fun retro feel.

On a slightly smaller scale, items such as herbs and spices can be given a similar treatment, with stylish storage making them worthy of being out on display. Likewise, when you are forced to display everything, try to ensure that the possessions you are displaying look good within themselves, too. This needn't mean spending huge sums of money: upgrade humdrum items by scouring second-hand stores for stacks of charming vintage linen dish towels and tablecloths, sturdy old enamel cookware, glass jars and cans to decant dry foods into, or even just unusual, attractive food packaging (try your local ethnic foodstore). The less stuff you feel needs hiding from sight, the easier curating the look of your space will be, and you'll be on to a winner.

ABOVE **Foodies' corner**
An old scaffolding plank, mounted on basic metal brackets, makes a characterful spot to store seasonings and spices, with cup hooks mounted underneath to create hanging space for pots and pans. A wall-mounted vintage wine crate provides a novel spot to store a collection of vintage kitchen linens.

LEFT **Small-scale storage**
Keep herbs and spices close to hand yet tucked away by storing them in an old glass cabinet sitting directly on a countertop.

MAKE YOUR OWN

Updating handles is a quick and easy way to change the look of a kitchen. However, that needn't necessarily mean buying new. For a quick fix, try simply wrapping the existing handles with some colored twine. Cut a generous length from your twine roll, and tie in a small knot at the bottom of your handle, butting up to the cabinet door. Then, working in the same direction, wrap the twine over the knot and the excess twine, pulling it taut as you go, slowly working your way up the handle until the whole thing is covered. When finished, tie the twine in a double knot at the top of the handle, with the knot head facing downward, and snip off the excess twine. For an alternative, you could cover the handles with colored tape or oilcloth fabric, both of which would also work on round handles (for the latter, cut a circle of fabric slightly larger than the handle, fold it around and tie it in place on the handle's spindle. Or, if you're handy (and are able to), simply remove the handles altogether and, using an adjustable hole saw drill bit, cut a small hole around 2 in (5 cm) in its place to create a finger hole.

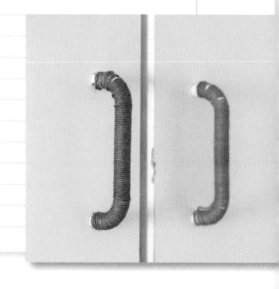

Often, just refreshing dirty grouting can make a huge difference to a tired kitchen space, and can be as simple as using a grout whitening pen, which costs very little and is readily available at DIY stores. Alternatively, for a bolder look, think about switching to a colored grout, which works especially well with plain white tiles. A swoosh of on-trend gray grout can transform tiles from so-so to super-smart, or try a fun pastel hue for an unexpected hint of color. Ensure the current grout is sound and scrape out any loose or flaking grout before starting.

Tile paint can also be used to hide a multitude of sins and is a much easier job than retiling. If you're renting a place with less-than-lovely tiles, consider asking your landlord for permission to do this; or, if you're a homeowner, this simple DIY job is a great tide-me-over if you can't afford to make costly changes to the space. Do it the easy way by simply painting straight over the tiles, or for a more authentic finish, scrape out the grout before starting, then reapply afterward so the grout lines are still visible.

If you want something less permanent, have a look at tile stickers. From designs that cover the whole tile (such as those used in the kitchen opposite) to cut-out motifs designed just to add design details on white tiles, this approach is perfect for the indecisive DIYer—fixed in place only with water, these stickers are removable without a trace. Alternatively, if you're handy with a saw and fancy a removable fix-up, pick up some plywood and cut it to the same size as your tiled area, then place this over your existing tiles, using heavy-duty stick-on Velcro strips for anchoring. Paint with a hardwearing wipeable paint, or even chalk paint, as seen here, for a look you can really have fun with.

BELOW **Handy spot**
A clipboard, tacked in place on a single nail, provides a useful spot to hold tear-out-and-keep recipes to hand.

RIGHT Green and gorgeous

This bold color choice adds interest and character, elevating an otherwise fairly basic kitchen into something far more special. New handles and vintage accessories complete the makeover. Wall-mounted coat hooks can be useful in the kitchen for holding anything from dish towels to cookie cutters, not just aprons.

BELOW Mid-century makeover

A coat of contrasting paint can work wonders on modernizing a piece of dark wood retro furniture. Remove doors and drawers before painting for a neater result. The retro-look barber board on the right makes a quirky noticeboard.

OPPOSITE Chalkboard calendar

Turn a painted chalkboard wall into a perpetual calendar by marking out squares with chalk or tape, and sticking adhesive numbers in each one to represent the days of the month.

Chalkboard makes a great surface elsewhere in a kitchen, too, thanks to its slightly textured, wipe-clean surface and the fact that it can be customized with drawings, notes, and shopping lists. But you can still get the look even if you're unable to paint, thanks to self-adhesive chalkboard sheets (usually found on a roll) or chalkboard stickers, which can be found in an array of shapes and sizes. Don't limit yourself to the walls either: consider using some chalkboard to transform dull appliances, such as a fridge or freezer, or even add it over flat-fronted cabinets. Similarly, colored contact paper or sticky-backed plastic can be a fantastic way to add a splash of color and interest to units as an alternative to painting them. To keep the look contemporary, avoid faux wood and marble effects in favor of block color.

If painting is an option, however, there's possibly no cheaper way to revive old cabinets. Give solid wooden doors a light sanding before applying a wood paint, priming if necessary (check the instructions on your paint can). If your cabinets are modern, chances are they will be constructed of chipboard covered in plastic, such as melamine, or a thin-wood veneer. These will require a specialist paint suitable for this surface type (as before, priming if necessary). Alternatively, if you'd rather skip the prepping, go for a specialist chalk-based paint—its slightly rougher, matte consistency should adhere to pretty much any surface, and will require just a top coat of wax or lacquer to make it resistant. The texture of paint on cabinets, with its visible brush strokes, alludes to quality and has a homespun charm: it can totally elevate the appearance of cheap plastic fronts. With all paint and coverings, always do a patch test first in an inconspicuous area, to make sure that the paint takes, or you can remove it without damaging what lies underneath.

Colored fairy lights at the window add to the informal feel of this kitchen

OPPOSITE Beautiful boiler

Disguise an ugly boiler in plain sight by covering its front with an offcut of wallpaper (keeping clear of ventilation points). Secure it into position with double-sided tape, or run decorative masking (Washi) tape around its edges.

RIGHT Cozy light

A mix-and-match casual artwork wall in the kitchen can be a good spot in which to hang less formal pieces you might not want on display in your main living areas. The casual arrangement shown here also helps the central heating dial, located in the middle of the wall, blend into the décor.

BELOW Transform white goods

A fridge door provides a blank canvas on which to tack up favorite postcards and images. Fix up with a mixture of cool magnets and decorative masking tape for a colorful display.

Art and mood lighting aren't often included as elements within a kitchen space, but they can in fact make a welcome distraction from other elements you may not be so keen on. Consider the durability of what you're using. While unframed artwork is best avoided, most framed pieces will be fine in a kitchen environment, and there's nothing to stop you having fun with small, inexpensive prints and postcards, too. An artwork wall can help the kitchen feel less of a solely functional space, particularly if it also serves as a dining room. Double up art as a disguise as well as a display, and take the concept of art in a less literal sense—think about using a print, dish towel, or even wallpaper to hide unsightly items, such as a boiler, as well as creating interest in the space.

As long as it's not too close to your sink, you can have a lamp in your kitchen. As well as illuminating gloomy corners, lighting is great for adding atmosphere. If existing task lighting is poor, consider having a work lamp with an adjustable head, so you can shine light where it's needed, or battery-operated push lights under wall units—an unobtrusive option, especially if power points are limited.

LEFT Cozy window nook

Mismatched fabrics enhance the comfy feel of this banquette, complemented by the pretty drinks bottles used as makeshift vases.

BELOW LEFT Stool seat

Decorate a basic wooden stool by gluing on strips of craft paper (these ones were leftover offcuts from other projects). Add a couple of coats of decorator's varnish on top to protect.

OPPOSITE Circles and squares

Checkerboard vinyl flooring is a cheap and effective option when renovating on a budget, and it makes a practical base for a kitchen. Consider it even if you're renting—cut to size and cheat by simply placing over your existing flooring, then secure at the edges with a hot glue gun. The glue can be scraped off and the flooring removed at a later date. Do a patch test first.

Regardless of whether you have a separate dining area or not, a seating nook within a kitchen is always a welcome spot for a hastily eaten breakfast, or simply a little area to take a breather, even if a single chair is all you have space for. You don't need to have a large kitchen with an island unit to squeeze in a breakfast bar—one can actually be squeezed into a relatively small space along a redundant wall, especially so if paired with stools that fit directly beneath it. An awkwardly shaped room might be best put to use with a small circular table in the corner, avoiding the need to fit anything into its tricky angles. A window seat can make a charming spot to sit and watch the world go by. Cheat your way to a built-in one by tracking down a storage box to fit inside any recesses, or to go in front of the window, then get some foam cut to fit the top, cover in fabric, and place a selection of comfy cushions on the top. A set of wooden mini steps can double as a little perching post for children, as well as being a handy aid to get to top shelves—choose or customize a colorful one to make the steps feel special.

Bare bulbs and
vintage-style flex
give a modern.
unfussy look

PRINTED BOOKPAGE *Wallpaper*

Wallpaper can be a great way to add pattern and personality to an otherwise plain kitchen, and while best avoided directly above a sink or stove, there's no reason to rule it out altogether. Try creating your own custom design, for a fraction of the cost of a designer roll. Just use the pages from unwanted old books, looking out for attractive fonts and slightly discolored paper, for an authentic vintage look, then print copyright-free images on them for a contemporary twist.

Renter's Alternatives

• Recreate this look using adhesive putty (Blu-Tack) or removable poster strips (and don't varnish over the top). Alternatively, paste your pages onto a large wooden board and lean it against the wall.

• To avoid printing the images yourself, consider alternative papers that are already patterned, such as comic books, vintage travel brochures, or interior magazines, for a quirky moodboard wall.

• For a different technique, involving fabric, place some cornstarch (cornflour) in a bowl and add a little boiling water, stirring as you go, slowly adding more water until you have a consistency similar to wallpaper paste. Let cool, then use the paste to stick the fabric to your walls, pasting it on with a paintbrush and smoothing it onto your walls. You can remove it without damaging the wall by dabbing it with a damp sponge and pulling down, though you should always do a patch test first.

1. Using a ruler and craft knife, cut out pages from books, ensuring you cut just a tiny distance away from the spine, to avoid including the spine's glue. Cut enough pages to cover your wall space.

2. For a free supply of images, go online and use a search engine such as Google to find copyright-free illustrations that are downloadable as high-resolution image files. Set up a folder on your desktop and build up enough to print onto every book page you want to use. Adjust your printer settings to accommodate this paper size (seeking online help if necessary), then print as many pages as you need.

3. Cover an old table with a wipe-clean plastic tablecloth and make sure that your chosen wall is completely clean and clear. Mix up some wallpaper paste, following the instructions on the packet.

4. Brush a little of the paste onto the back of your first print, then stick it at one edge of the area that is being decorated. Continue to work across the space as best you can, fitting in the pages as neatly as possible and using a credit card to smooth out any bubbles.

5. Continue across the area, allowing each page to overlap to varying degrees—ideally you want to finish at the other side with a page that just fits the remaining space. Move onto the next line, continuing until the whole area is covered.

6. For areas more likely to encounter wear and tear, such as a kitchen, add a coat of decorator's varnish to protect the walls. Test in an inconspicuous corner first before covering the whole wall.

A vintage educational poster adds a charming, homey touch to this plain wall

However grand or bijou your dining space, it doesn't take much effort to create an attractive, usable area, whatever the available room may be. Whether it's part of your kitchen, tucked into a corner of a living space, or even has a dedicated room of its own, this is an area with which you can afford to have a little fun. Whether the space is for family meals or entertaining, or is just an extra spot in which to sit and read or work, try to make yours an area you wish to spend time in, mealtime or not, by filling it with personality and homey touches.

If you're setting up the space from scratch, undoubtedly a table and some chairs will be your biggest expense. Think about what will fit best within your space—even the smallest of alcoves can usually accommodate some type of table, whether it's a fold-down variety attached to a wall, or a gate-leg table that can be tucked away almost flat if there isn't space to keep it out all the time. Foldable chairs are a good bet for such a scenario, allowing you to store them in a cupboard (or even behind the sofa) when not in use. If you have the space for a table to be out full-time, look for extendable pieces to offer the widest flexibility. A rustic farmhouse-style rectangular table can look fabulous in many different settings, particularly when teamed with chairs of a contrasting style, but if your room is more of a square shape, you may find that a circular model best fits the space. Forget the notion (and expense) of buying a matching set of chairs, and pick up an eclectic collection of singles or doubles as funds allow. If your budget won't stretch to a table you really love, look for a freebie locally or online, then cover it with a cloth until you can afford something more to your taste.

DINING SPACES
Eating, socializing, and relaxing

MAKE YOUR OWN

Dated dark brown furniture can be given a new lease of life with a lick of bright paint, but why not personalize it even further? The owner of this family hand-me-down unit was keen to continue its sense of history in a way that suited how the family live now, by pasting on color-tinted photography printouts of every family member for a unique look. Create something similar inside a door recess by cutting out your printouts then coating both sides in white craft glue, watering it down if it's too gloopy. Place them on the cabinet and leave to dry, wiping away any excess glue with the brush. Fill in the gaps with colorful paper circles in coordinating hues and paint on a few extra coats of glue, allowing them to dry between each layer, to give added protection. For an extra twist, the old handles have been removed and replaced with colorful beads, threaded onto wire and poked through the existing handle holes, then twisted together inside to fasten.

Storage cubes make the most of wasted space at the end of this table, keeping it clear of clutter and providing a home for favorite teas, and are easy to move when extra tabletop space is needed.

BELOW **Cozy feel**
Despite nothing matching in this space style-wise, the warm, homely feel of the pieces on show tie the look together beautifully.

If your kitchen is lacking in units, the dining room can store extra kitchen bits and bobs. Dining rooms have long been used to house related items, such as dinner services, but see how else you can maximize the space with the inclusion of cooking oils, bowls of fruit and vegetables, and even fresh potted herbs. Occasional items, like baking equipment, often fit better in a cabinet here, rather than take up valuable kitchen space. Built-in storage can be costly, so make the most of what you have access to, from freestanding old cabinets to wooden storage crates. Mesh- or ladder-sided shelving can be especially useful to make the most of storage potential—pop a few butcher's hooks down the side for hanging additional items, such as cooking implements and string vegetable bags.

Don't forget the décor, too: the dining table is one of the easiest items to transform immediately, simply by throwing over a tablecloth. If you prefer a more fitted look, cut a piece of oilcloth fabric slightly larger than the tabletop, and staple it around the underside of the table's lip to create a wipe-down fitted surface that can easily be removed without a trace by simply removing the staples. For the floor, while a deep pile rug wouldn't be appropriate in such a space, a woven design could add comfort; alternatively, for a more vibrant look, consider an outdoor plastic rug, which can be inexpensive and available in an array of patterns and designs. To spread out the cost, buy several smaller rugs and layer them up as you can afford them, rather than opting for one large design.

Thinking of your walls as part of your storage can be wise in a small space, as long as you are able to take advantage of them. High shelves can be a great way to store away items that aren't in constant use, as well as to display favorite collections: a dining room makes a perfect home to store that set of old tea pots or vintage cake stands, for example. Placing shelves in an alcove and finishing with a chest of drawers underneath does the same job as a buffet unit, without having to deal with heavy, cumbersome furniture. Add some drawer organizers to facilitate storing cutlery and serveware, then lower drawers can be left to store spare table linens and dish towels. To blend in any furniture, paint it the same color as your walls to help it to disappear, so to speak, or simply embrace a mismatched aesthetic and leave things as you find them. If you like the natural patina of old wooden pieces but feel yours are getting a little grubby, rub in some beeswax with a cloth to restore a little of their former grandeur.

ABOVE Pull up a seat
If floor space is limited but ceiling height isn't, fix up a couple of hooks to hang spare chairs from. Fold-down designs will encroach into the space even less and can look like a feature in their own right.

OPPOSITE Playing shop
Beginning life as a shop display unit, this freestanding unit works brilliantly in a small dining space. The slim ledge of a transom window makes for a fun place to display freestanding foam letters.

RIGHT Find a sunny spot
Plant cuttings live happily in this sunny nook and decoratively do the same job as flowers, without the repeat costs. Colorful mini bottles lined up along the window ledge create a jewel-like feel when the sun shines through them.

A lichen-covered branch, used in place of flowers, comes to life when placed in front of dark walls, and toy racing horses from a vintage game look witty placed "running" along the table

A fruit rack hanging from the ceiling makes clever use of this space

PREVIOUS PAGE
Sumptuous color

This luxurious, inky-blue feature wall is the perfect foil for an otherwise relatively simple and modest setting. Despite its somewhat grand appearance, this dining space is actually squeezed into the corner of a living room, proving that size and style are not always interlinked.

LEFT Supersize wall décor

This stunning giant mural, featuring an iconic image by photographer Slim Aarons, provides a great talking point. Elements of its design are picked up throughout the room, such as the vibrant rug in cool blues and greens.

RIGHT TV camouflage

This wall-mounted television is perfectly disguised among a wall of artwork, when set against dark paint. Be bold when it comes to gallery walls: this example is filled from floor to ceiling, and bright punches of color are used throughout.

As an entertaining space, you can be a little bolder with color and pattern in a dining room, and if your dining area is within another room, a different wall treatment can help to demarcate it from the rest of the space. Whether it's through quirky artworks, bold color and pattern, or even a striking mural, this is an area in which to indulge in your more playful side. Removable wallpapers and wall stickers have grown immensely in popularity in recent years, in part thanks to a rise in renters and the reluctance of homeowners to do anything controversial to their properties for risk of affecting a future sale. The result is myriad choices of designs, from repeat patterns to large-scale murals that can be pasted onto a flat wall and simply peeled off to remove when no longer required. In an otherwise plain and featureless room, this mural turns the space from bland to show-stopping, and although a mural of this size doesn't come cheap, its incredibly bold design means that little else is needed to decorate the room.

OPPOSITE Gloriously retro

Make a statement while you store and serve your drinks. Alternatively, such a trolley would work well storing baskets of fruit and vegetables.

RIGHT Clusters of style

Create more kitchen and dining storage inexpensively with wall-mounted shelves and storage bars, rather than bulky cabinets. A spare chair can be put to good use holding cookery books, and is easily cleared when extra guests visit.

As well as being popular due to their looks, the resounding appeal of pieces of retro furniture is down to their hardwearing nature. If a piece of furniture has already been around for 60 years, you can be confident that it's unlikely to break anytime soon. Increasingly, more and more items that had fallen out of favor in recent years have seen a rise in popularity, and are being rediscovered by a new generation. The drinks trolley, long considered the height of kitsch, is one such item worthy of a revisit. Compact and portable, it provides a handy two-tiered surface to hold glasses and napkins as well as drinks, and looks novel in a dining room. Sideboards, too, can hold a large array of items without requiring any fixings to walls, and can often be found cheaply at second-hand shops. When tied in with modern pieces, they really can provide the best of both worlds.

DECORATIVE *Clad Shelving*

Add color and pattern in the most unexpected of areas in your home by personalizing shelving with some decorative fruit-crate cladding. While chunky vintage crates can command a premium, many local markets use much thinner "disposable" versions, made from low-grade wood, which can often be found going begging at the end of market day. Their fruit- and veg-related designs give a quirky yet relevant touch to a kitchen or dining area.

You Will Need:

Shelving with appropriate brackets (see step 1 for guidance)

Spirit level

Pencil

Tape measure

Electric drill with relevant sizes of drill bits, screws, and screw anchors (wall plugs) (see step 3 for guidance)

Hammer

Screwdriver

Thin wooden fruit crates—enough to cover the length of your shelves when cut up

Wood saw or hacksaw

General-purpose sandpaper

Clear matte varnish, suitable for wood

Paintbrush

Wood glue

Old cloth

NOTE: Ensure that all of your drill bits, screws, and screw anchors (wall plugs) are appropriate for your wall type—if in doubt, ask an expert for advice.

1. You may already have some shelves you could clad, but if not, look out for either "floating" shelf kits or standard shelves with brackets, both of which should be readily available in DIY stores. If you prefer, create your own by visiting a DIY store with a wood-cutting facility, and get them to cut you some MDF (medium-density fiberboard) to your desired size, then team it with brackets. Make sure your fronts are totally flat, and are ideally at least 1in (2.5cm) thick.

2. Using a spirit level, pencil, and tape measure, mark onto your walls where your brackets need to go. With a standard shelf, ensure your brackets will give adequate support for the weight of its proposed contents, and evenly space them around 8 in (20 cm) from either end, using an extra middle bracket if the shelves are quite long. The brackets for a floating shelf, however, will be concealed within its body.

3. Fit the electric drill with an appropriate drill bit, then make fixing holes in the wall. Insert your screw anchors into them (tapping with a hammer to ease them into the wall) before screwing the brackets into place. Fix the shelf into position, securing it with small screws through the underside of each bracket (if required).

4. Once your shelves are in place, turn your attention to your wooden fruit crates. Mark on each crate with a pencil which lengths you would like to use, then, using a saw, carefully cut free these sections. Repeat until you have enough lengths to cover the front of your shelves, laying the pieces out as you go to check the overall design. Next, sand the ends of each length to remove rough edges, then brush off the sawdust. In a well-ventilated area, lay out your lengths, then brush two coats of clear matte varnish over the fronts and edges of each length. Leave to dry.

5. Starting from one end, take your first length and run a line of wood glue near its top (or all over, if your lengths are the same height as your shelf thickness). Press into position at one end of the shelf, lining up the top of the box length flush with the shelf top, with any overhang at the bottom of the shelf. Wipe off any glue leaking out from the edges. Hold into place for a couple of minutes until dry.

6. Repeat the process with each length, working systematically from one side to the other. Leave to form a strong bond overnight before using the shelves.

Renter's Alternatives

● Look out for vintage-style fruit and veg stickers that you could place straight over the fronts of existing shelving (or even furniture). Cut to size and secure in place with adhesive putty (Blu-Tack) or removable poster strips.

● Stick a line of colorful ribbon or trimming to shelf fronts for a splash of color with some double-sided tape (test in a small corner first to ensure it comes off cleanly without damaging the wood).

● To add more texture, think about adding some 3D objects, such as a line of buttons, some children's small plastic construction blocks, or even old jigsaw puzzle pieces. If you're able, use a hot glue gun to fix them down, but if not, adhesive putty again makes a good reversible option.

Chapter Three

BEDROOMS AND BATHROOMS

Relaxing and luxurious boutique hotel-style BEDROOMS and BATHROOMS often top the style wishlists of many home owners. Usually these are the only parts of the house that are truly private, so the concept of wanting them to feel like a sanctuary, in whatever guise, is nothing new. But in a home-for-now, the bedroom might also have to double up as a home office or nursery, or it might not even be a separate room at all. And as renters' average ages continue to rise, it's not uncommon to be sharing a bathroom with housemates well into your 30s and beyond. Rather than baulk in horror, embrace the simple touches you can add in order to get just a hint of that luxury feel.

Plastic storage pockets, mounted on the wall, come in handy for holding small accessories such as sunglasses, cameras, and cellphone chargers

A more intimate space than other rooms in the house, the bedroom is often the place to try out a more personal decorating approach. Arguably the focal point of any bedroom, the bed is luckily an easy item to dress up, whatever your budget. Forget the notion of perfectly coordinated bedlinen sets with matching throws and cushions, and piece together your own look. If you're not sure where to start, opt for simple white bedlinen, teamed with a gorgeous throw, blanket, or even a pretty tablecloth, and take that as your starting point. If you're after a bit more color, you could even customize your own bedlinen by part-dying it to create an ombre effect, sewing on a pompom trim for decoration, or even using fabric paint and stencils to create your own pattern.

   This tiny bedroom, actually tucked into a disused porch, is barely any bigger than the bed itself. Rather than try to disguise its size by sticking to neutrals, its owners have embraced its bijou proportions and used them to create a cozy, interesting nook, thanks to its bold walls and mismatched bedding. Wall-mounted storage compensates for lack of floor space, and a mosquito net teamed with wall-mounted fairy lights gives an ethereal feel (as well as protecting sleepers from insect bites during summer months).

BEDROOMS
A restful place to relax

Sometimes the simplest schemes are the best, and more than any other room, the bedroom should feel restful, providing a retreat from the rest of your property and, indeed, the wider world. White walls create, quite literally, the perfect blank canvas on which to layer accessories, soft furnishings, and artwork, for a relaxed and cozy space that's free of clutter and easy to change around without redecorating. Often the largest item in the room, the bed itself can provide a wealth of storage opportunities. If you're in the market for a new bed, consider a model with a lift-up mattress on a hydraulic mechanism, which offers more storage than any other type of bed. While not the cheapest option, it may mean that you don't need to invest in as much storage furniture elsewhere in the room, providing a saving in that way. A cheaper alternative, the divan, is also a worthy contender, but to avoid scrimping on the style stakes, keep its base covered with a simple valance, or even just tuck some fabric over the bottom to disguise it. For beds on legs, there are myriad storage boxes and baskets built with this purpose in mind,

ABOVE Cast a glow

This dark, north-facing bedroom gets a magical lift after nightfall when its ceiling-hanging festoon lights are turned on and the wood-paneled ceiling, painted gold, bounces light throughout the room.

RIGHT Simple space

An adjustable wall-mounted light provides an easy-to-maneuver light source: a great option if you don't have space for a night table. The nearly bare walls are furnished simply with a favorite postcard, casually tacked above the bed.

but try a more imaginative solution: old suitcases or large vintage cans will work just as well, and are more aesthetically pleasing if visible from the room.

If your room does serve another function, such as doubling up as a home office, try to tuck this area away in a corner (an alcove is ideal) and think about ways in which you can disguise it when not in use. Options to consider are placing it in a cupboard with a door or pull-down shutter to hide everything away at the end of the day, or placing a curtain or screen in front of it, to act as a room divider. Restoring the bedroom to its original function, free from visual distraction, should aid your sleep.

ABOVE **Sloped ceiling**
Don't be afraid of empty space. Placing this crucifix in a room with a pitched ceiling gives an almost cathedral-like feel, despite its more modest proportions.

If you can't get enough of color, even in the bedroom, make sure it doesn't overpower the room by using it with consideration. Rather than making a small space feel smaller, it can actually help to unite it and create a cozy, considered mood. Avoid any overly dominant hues within a small space and opt for warm tones for a more welcoming feel. Accessories should coordinate, in the loosest sense of the word: choose pieces that you love and that have some form of theme that links them all together, be it color tones, pattern, or simply texture.

ABOVE LEFT Comfy cushions

Envelope cushions are super easy to make, and are a great way to use up fabric offcuts. The floral motif featured throughout these cushions and duvet cover helps tie the look together, despite their differing styles.

LEFT Studio sofabed

Thanks to savvy styling, the sofabed in this studio space can be easily transformed from day to night use. By using bed pillows as armrests and tucking the duvet over the back, everything is at hand to transform it back into a bed at night-time, yet stylish enough to feel like a "normal" living room during the day.

MAKE YOUR OWN

It makes sense, storage-wise, to use the largest wardrobe you can fit into your bedroom, particularly if you have lots of clothes and shoes.

To stop such a large piece feeling overpowering, painting it can be a good idea, but if you want to make it more of a talking point, consider adding some stripes. Black and white has a timeless look and will go with any other colors in the room; or for something less bold, stick to colors that are closer in tone. To get a perfect stripe, try the following decorator's trick: paint the whole unit first in the lighter color (after preparing and priming your piece as necessary for furniture of its type) then, when dry, place strips of low-tack decorator's masking tape on it, either side of where you want your darker stripes to be. Use a tape measure or plumb line to keep the lines straight. Then, inside the sections earmarked for your dark stripes, first add more of your base paint over the area where the tape meets the wood, and let dry. When you go to paint on your dark stripes over the top, you will find that your lines are much crisper, as any paint "bleeding" under the tape will have occurred with the lighter base paint, and will therefore not be visible.

OPPOSITE Paint transformation

A dated glossy pine chest of drawers is transformed with these bold color choices in an otherwise neutral space. Painting the drawer handles a contrasting color gives a fun twist, or you could replace the handles with mismatched new ones for an eclectic look.

RIGHT Creating divides

As well as utilizing an awkward space well, hanging clothes like this also creates an impermanent room divider, semi-concealing the bedroom from the rest of the apartment. An internal curtain can be pulled across when inside the room to create a cozy hideaway at bedtime.

BELOW Boxy room

Rather than boxing in the joists from the mezzanine level above, here they have been left on show for a slightly industrial look.

Sometimes, a clever use of space is needed to create a bedroom environment where there is no dedicated bedroom. Whether done with a transformative sofabed, as seen on page 110, or tucked into a nook, like the porchway bedroom shown at the start of this section, a little creative thinking can lead to a solution. Here, the void under a mezzanine within an open-plan live/work unit has been transformed into a sleeping sanctuary thanks to some clever tricks, many of which could be applied to a more standard type of property. As the bedroom nook has limited natural light, walls have been kept white, and the room is adorned with pops of color in the form of decorative hanging mobiles, framed art prints, and a brightly painted cabinet. Two wooden poles, one suspended from the other, form a makeshift wardrobe, attached to a beam on two hooks. This utilizes a gap that wouldn't have been able to accommodate a standard wardrobe or clothes rail. The remainder of the bedroom storage spills out into the hallway (in shoe cubby holes running along the wall and a brightly painted chest of drawers), but it certainly doesn't feel as though it is bursting out of the room.

LEFT Skaterboy

For a super-cool look for an older child, broken skateboards are used as a display above the bed, along with vintage oil drums used for storage. Old skateboards can also make excellent and unusual shelves when supported on shelf brackets.

With housing costs spiraling, it can be increasingly difficult for families to get their forever home. That doesn't mean that children's rooms need necessarily be a compromise, however. Keeping walls neutral and adding color with furniture and accessories is a great way to add interest without creating an overly childlike space that might concern your landlord or put off future buyers when you come to sell. If children have to share rooms, a bunk bed is the best space-saving option. Make it feel like an adventure by cladding one with curtains, to create their own special hideaway. Involve kids in the décor, allowing them space to curate their own displays of favorite rock collections or dinosaur toys. Ensure the space has enough storage to keep things under control, without stifling their creativity.

ABOVE Repurposed drawer shelves

Salvaged drawers from a broken unit have been cleverly upcycled into shelves by placing them on their sides and screwing them into the wall. Create a similar look without the drilling by using freestanding crates. A colorful curtain helps to hide toys and clutter in a corner.

ABOVE RIGHT Room for two

Despite sharing a room, these bunk beds have an individual feel to them, thanks to the incorporation of photos of each child in each bunk, along with personally chosen cushions and toys. Storage boxes under the bed are smartened up with a blanket to cover them, in place of a valance.

RIGHT Color and pattern

Plain furniture is given a child-friendly (and adult-friendly) makeover by painting cupboards in bright hues and adding panels of retro wallpaper for a cheery look. A plain white shade (blind) has had interest added with a red felt trim.

BELOW Wrapped in ribbon

A painted canvas makes for a pretty headboard, tying in with the artworks above. Here, ribbon is the perfect disguise for a less-than-lovely light cord and bare lampshade. By wrapping various pieces throughout both, they have been turned into a focal point in their own right. This technique could be applied to any cord, especially when rewiring with more interesting colored or vintage flex isn't an option.

BELOW Smart stripes

A reclaimed piece of wood has been simply propped up in front of this bed's existing headboard, with the mattress and pillows holding it in place. Strips of extra-wide decorative masking tape, designed for adding pattern to walls, look smart in stripes. A simple chair makes a good alternative to a night (bedside) table.

The headboard can really be the cherry on the cake when it comes to bedroom styling, helping to frame the bed and making the most of the dead space above it. If you don't already have one, try out a few alternative ideas. Simply placing a large, flat item, such as an artist's stretched canvas, a piece of wood, or some old shutters behind the bed, and using the weight of the bed itself to hold it in place, may be all it takes to create that focal interest. A large fabric hanging, or even a couple of drops of wallpaper visually do the same job. If you're feeling crafty, mock up a headboard design by sketching an outline above your bed, then filling it in with paint (or even wallpaper scraps cut to fit). Alternatively, simply use a massed collection of artworks in a rectangular formation to fill in the gap. If you do have a headboard that you're not keen on, however, see what you can do to disguise it. Paint can be transformative to any frame (if it's metal, look out for enamel paints, which often come in an array of colors, or use a chalk-based paint, which should adhere to any surface). To turn a hard headboard into a soft one, cut a piece of foam to the same size, then wrap it in fabric, folding it around the sides and top, then fix in place at the back with safety pins for a removable makeover.

If you don't have space for night (bedside) tables, a slim shelf running around about 3 ft (1 m) above the bed could act as both a focal point and a nightstand for bedside drinks and books as well as somewhere to display decorative items. If your bed is on wheels, you could even position it in front of a shallow storage unit, using the visible areas for display and the covered section to store lesser-used items, such as guest bedding.

ABOVE **Homemade headboard**
Made by the owner, using a sheet of MDF, this headboard cost a fraction of what a similar store-bought design would have been. After the foam-covered headboard was wrapped in wadding and then had fabric wrapped around it, it was hung directly from the wall by screws in its back, suspended on wall-mounted D hooks.

ABOVE Customized nightstand

This generous nightstand has been "Ikea hacked" by its owner, by
spraypainting it in a vibrant blue paint, adding brass campaign handles,
and screwing on corner braces as décor. If you have the space, a small
chest of drawers would work just as well for a similar look.

ABOVE Bedside crate

Reading material is kept close at hand in this crate, which doubles up as both storage and a nightstand. A modern lamp in a vibrant color provides an interesting juxtaposition of styles.

ABOVE MIDDLE Suspended shelf

A small floating shelf makes a good alternative to a nightstand when the floor space is needed for other things, like housing this pouffe. An oversized tissue paper rose means you will always wake up to flowers.

ABOVE RIGHT Clever cover-up

If you're not keen on a piece of furniture, or it's your landlord's and you can't change it, try covering it with a cloth: here, an old tablecloth hides a less-than-desirable bedside cabinet, without blocking access to its drawers. Free up space on a cabinet by attaching a clamp spotlight to your bedframe, as shown.

RIGHT Telephone table

With no space for a floor-standing night (bedside) table, this old wall-mounted telephone stand is perfect for keeping bedside bits and bobs close to hand.

RIGHT Crafty dressing table

An old Singer folding sewing table, complete with original machine still tucked away safely inside, is put to better use as a whimsical dressing table with a piece of linen draped over the top and a mirror balanced in its center.

BELOW Book club

Utilize the tops of furniture, too: with no room for a bookcase, this provides a great space to stack paperbacks as well as display larger ornaments.

"Repurposing" and "upcycling" are real buzzwords in the interiors world right now. Whether reassigning an item's intended use (repurposing) or transforming a piece that is no longer fit for purpose into something totally new (upcycling), there is lots you can do to get things working for you. And by thinking in this way, you can cut down on new furniture costs, as well as saving space by using a single item for a dual purpose. Try something as simple as making an old wardrobe work twice as hard by fitting a second hanging rail halfway down it, to double your hanging storage for tops (keep any longer pieces together at one end and just hook behind the lower rail). Alternatively, simply reuse something originally intended for use elsewhere, such as an antique radio cabinet taking the part of a night (bedside) table. Keep an open mind and think beyond the boundaries of each room.

MAKE YOUR OWN

Converting an existing piece of furniture, by adding extra storage beneath it, is a far more cost-effective alternative to buying something new. Here, a fabric skirt was added underneath a dressing table to create storage for shoes, hidden underneath on a freestanding shoe rack. To make your own table skirt, take some fabric around 6 in (15 cm) longer than your table, and cut into four panels: two to cover either end and two to act like standard curtains, joining in the middle across the front. Ensure the fabric is around one and a half times wider than the furniture so that it gathers nicely. Hem the sides, then sew a channel along the top and insert some curtain wire into this, cut slightly

shorter than the width of the two sides and the front section. Taking some hook and eyes that fit the wire, wind the hooks into the end of each length of wire and fix hooks into the inner side and front corners of your furniture, drilling a pilot hole first if necessary. Hang into position to check the final length, then where the excess fabric length touches the floor, fold up on the underside to create your hem length and pin into place. Take down to sew the bottom hem before rehanging.

LEFT Tucked-away shelving

With no space for a wardrobe in this tiny bedroom, clothes are instead stored in stacks on shelves, inside an old boiler cuboard.

BELOW Model your accessories

A collection of scarves and brooches needn't be hidden away: a vintage mannequin makes a great perching spot for them to be stuck into and draped over. A smaller child mannequin will take up less space than a full-sized model.

LEFT `A midas touch`

A basic clothes rail has been given a glamorous makeover with some gold spraypaint. Adding inexpensive kitchen shelves above it and spraying the brackets gold to match make the most of this space for both storage and display.

BELOW `Flexible and hidden`

A cubby area or corner of a room can easily be converted into a wardrobe space with the addition of basic metal bars fixed to the wall on shelf brackets. A fun curtain masks off the space.

Clothing often proves the biggest storage challenge within a bedroom. If space or furniture is limited, adapt: arrange clothes in neat piles on shelves if hanging space is in short supply, or likewise place a chest of drawers inside a wardrobe to make use of redundant hanging space at the bottom, which as a bonus would also free up the floor space it would otherwise occupy. And if you don't have room to hide things, why not display them instead? Use favorite clothes, jewelry, and accessories as part of your décor, both creating a style statement and diminishing the need for extra storage. From displaying a special dress on a hanger at the side of a wardrobe, to arranging bags in color order along an open shelf, or stacking up bangles in cylindrical vases or pots, have fun with your treasures and create a system that works for you and gives you room to grow.

ABOVE Dressing table detail

An old brandy glass keeps a collection of rings tidy and easy to select while also providing a pretty detail on a dressing table.

RIGHT Repurpose a bookcase

There's no reason why a bookcase should be used to store just books. In lieu of fitted shelving, it makes a stylish and practical place to arrange shoes, jewelry, and handbags. A well-honed styling eye ensures that everything looks chic. Removing the bottom shelf provides the height needed to store boots.

UPCYCLED *Jewelry Hooks*

Don't hide away your favorite jewelry—make a feature of it with this striking hook set. Requiring only basic DIY skills, this project provides maximal storage with minimal wall damage. You will need some vintage sterling silver spoons, which you can buy quite cheaply at thrift or charity shops and vintage fairs. Look for a hallmark to ensure they are sterling silver rather than stainless steel, which will be much harder to work with.

You Will Need:

Scrap wood batten, in a suitable height and length for your hooks

Wood saw, if required (see step 1)

General-purpose sandpaper, if required (see step 1)

White spirit and an old cloth

Water-based emulsion paint in a color of your choice

Paint brush

Selection of vintage sterling silver spoons—either a matching set or different shapes and sizes

Pencil and eraser

Tape measure

Drill with small metal pilot-hole wood drill bits (see steps 4 and 7 for guidance)

Masking tape, if required (optional)

Broom handle or thick piece of dowel

Pliers and an old cloth, if needed (see step 5)

Countersunk wood screws and cup washers that fit (see steps 3, 9, and 10 for guidance)

Screwdriver

Two silver sugar tongs (optional)

1. If your scrap wood is longer than required, cut it down with the saw and sand the rough edges. Then, if the front of the wood is uneven, smooth it off with sandpaper, dust it clean, and wipe with some white spirit on an old cloth.

2. When dry, paint the front and sides of the batten with some water-based emulsion (some leftover paint from another project, or a tester pot, would be ideal for this). Keep the brush strokes light so that you can still see the grain and texture of the wood through the paint. Let dry.

3. Plan the best way to use your screws and spoons. The screws need to be long enough to go through the spoons when they are facing down and into most of the depth of the batten, but they should not be particularly thick. Ensure you have enough spoons to provide all the hooks you require, plus two identical spare spoons, which will be used to form decorative wall fixings for hanging the finished item.

4. Use the unpainted side of the batten as a surface to drill on to protect your tabletop. Rest a spoon, facing down, onto the batten and hold it firmly in place by pressing down on its handle. Using your drill and a metal drill bit of the appropriate width for your screw, make a hole in the center of the spoon head (or two holes, one above the other, with a gap between them, for a bigger spoon). If you're finding this difficult, stick a strip of masking tape down the center of the spoon head, to alleviate any slipping. Check that the screw fits through the hole—if it's too small, use the next largest drill bit. Repeat with the other spoons.

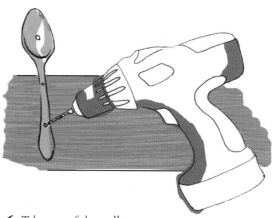

5. Take one of the spoons that you're going to use for the hooks and gently bend the handle backward to form the hook shape. Bending it round a broom handle or piece of doweling will help to achieve an even curve. Repeat for the remaining spoons. (Do not bend the two spoons for the wall fixings.) If you're struggling to bend any spoons, use some pliers, covering the spoon with an old cloth first to protect against scratches.

6. Take one of the wall-fixing spoons. Hold it in position and mark two holes to be drilled—one a short distance down from the spoon head and the other closer to the end of the handle. Drill the two holes, again using the unpainted side of the batten as a drilling surface, then repeat for the other wall-fixing spoon.

Renter's Alternatives

- Avoid drilling into walls by fixing the hook board directly into the side of a wooden piece of your own furniture that you don't mind making a couple of holes in.

- Lean a large piece of wood against your wall on top of a desk or dressing table, and screw your spoons into this. Place something heavy in front of the board to stop it from slipping down.

- Skip the DIY and purchase an over-the-door coat rack to hang up your jewelry.

7. Place your hooks on the right side of the batten, working out where you would like each one to be positioned. Measure to ensure they are regularly spaced, and an even distance from the bottom of the batten. Switch to a pilot-hole wood drill bit, then, carefully holding each spoon in place, create pilot holes by drilling through the holes in each spoon and into the batten beneath them.

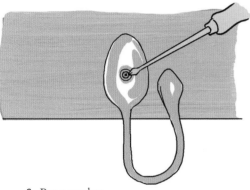

8. Put a washer onto each screw, then screw through each hook and into the batten below, until secure, continuing until the row is complete. Flip the piece over.

9. On the reverse side of the wood, place each wall-fixing spoon around 2 in (5 cm) in from either end, with the spoon head protruding clear of the top of the wood, facing upward. As before, drill a pilot hole through the holes in each spoon handle, and fix into place with some slightly shorter screws. (Washers aren't necessary here as they are simply for a neater finish.)

10. For extra decoration, you could add a pretty sugar tong over each end—if you can find one that's about the width of your batten, it will cling snugly to the wood without needing to be fixed into place.

11. Hold the finished piece against a wall and decide where you want to hang it, then poke a screw through the holes in the head of each wall-fixing spoon, to make a mark where you want the holes to be. Using the appropriate drill bit, screws (and screw anchors or wall plugs, if required) for your wall, create your holes and screw into position.

KEEP YOUR

TEETH CLEAN

A cluster of artworks helps
the toiletries cabinet blend
into the background

BATHROOMS
Creating a sanctuary

Like its functional friend the kitchen, the bathroom can notoriously be the most difficult space to transform in a home-for-now. For renters, there is little chance of changing major items such as sanitaryware, and as a full bathroom refurbishment can run into the thousands, it's not a job for the faint-hearted. But with a trusty toolkit of tricks and some strategic planning, and by employing small accent pieces and removable items, you'd be surprised what a difference you can make.

While many things in the home can be disguised in one form or another, the actual bathroom suite itself is one thing that, sadly, cannot. So if yours comes in a dated color palette, try instead to embrace its retro charm by bringing in touches of its color in simple modern accents throughout the room to balance things out, rather than simply ignoring it. There can be a certain appeal to (some) retro fixtures, and even the much-derided avocado suite has been quietly making a comeback for a few years now, as a backlash to the now-ubiquitous white suite. But for the rest of the room, you can unleash your imagination. As seen on page 80, tile stickers and tile paint can be used to almost instantly transform tired old tiles, as can a simple freshen-up with a grout whitening pen. Look out for quirky shower curtain designs, or add some decadence to the space with a homemade fabric shower curtain; as long as you retain a plastic inner curtain for lining, you can really make a feature of the bathtub with some pretty fabric allowed to hang down over its front. If bath paneling is letting the room down, see if you can replace it with a new one, or fix on some simple tongue-and-groove battens, using the existing timber frame sub-structure to attach it to, if you're handy with a saw. If your bathroom's existing flooring has seen better days, some cheap vinyl flooring could instantly smarten things up and is easy to install yourself, to tide you through your tenancy (or until you can afford something better). If the existing floor is flat and sound, you can simply lay the vinyl over the top, securing the edges with a hot glue gun.

ABOVE **Natural display**

A collection of stones and shells looks striking when displayed in a simple vase or jar. Keep the look clean, or mix in a few cheap gift-store shell ornaments for an element of kitsch.

OPPOSITE **Moody blues**

The dark tones of this room create a cozy, comforting look, perfect for a bathing space.

Painting can be a great way to pull a bathroom scheme together if the room does have a colored suite or tiles, and it will provide an alternative focus for the room, therefore helping to detract from the fittings. Likewise, if the room is otherwise plain with white tiles and sanitaryware, seize the opportunity to inject some personality into it. Dark paint, as seen here, adds a real sense of drama, and if you're reluctant to use bold or dark shades elsewhere in the home, the bathroom could be the perfect place to test the waters. Ensure you use a bathroom-appropriate paint that will stand up to humidity, and wash down the walls thoroughly before starting, using a specialist primer if necessary. If you're finding bathroom paint color choices limited, look for a paint manufacturer who can mix up a color in your preferred hue, made with a paint base appropriate for bathroom use. A matte or low-sheen finish will give you a more sophisticated, period look, while paint with a higher gloss content may be easier to wipe clean.

There's no reason you can't decorate bathroom walls with artworks, and it can be a clever way to add interest to an otherwise plain space. If your room suffers from condensation, keep any precious prints for other rooms, however, and stick to more cheap-and-cheerful pieces, or photos you can reprint if needed. Alternatively, hang items that are impervious to condensation, like a collection of pretty mismatched vintage plates. Beach finds, such as shells and pebbles, are a great way to loosen the sometimes clinical feel of bathrooms, and can often serve as mementoes of beachside walks and special holidays. You could carry on the natural theme by adding a statement mirror with a rustic wooden frame, or indulge in a spot of glamor with an ornate, carved gilt design: look out for options at antiques fairs and if they are particularly big and heavy, simply lean one up against the wall rather than damage walls with fixings.

Artwork needn't always be originally intended to hang on the wall—this pretty butterfly print is framed giftwrap

BELOW Spray it bright

A cheap metal industrial-style unit, spraypainted
in a vibrant color, adds a fun touch to the bathroom
and will cope well with condensation, too.

Matching towel sets
can be expensive, so
build up a collection of
mismatched vintage
ones, instead, which look
good enough to go out
on display

Storage can often be an issue in bathrooms, and nothing lets down its look more than a clutter of bottles and beauty products, not to mention making it harder to clean. Retailers offer all sorts of purpose-designed furniture pieces for such a space, but you needn't limit yourself to their selection. An old nightstand could easily be squeezed into a corner, providing storage beneath and a display space above. A CD tower makes great use of a slim recess: remove some of its shelves to provide a mixture of tall and short storage to accommodate bottles of differing heights. Laundry baskets could just as well be used to store clean towels, or even toilet rolls. Alternatively, displaying towels rolled up in an open basket not only gives a boutique hotel look but also takes up less space than if they were folded.

Items such as ladders can often be difficult to store in a small apartment. If you don't have anywhere to hide one, make it a feature instead. Track down a characterful wooden A-frame ladder and, when it's not needed for official ladder duties, use it to store towels and bottles. A leaning ladder would look just as good, and if floor space is tight, it can be wall-mounted on a couple of hooks. This would also work well in the bedroom to store high-heeled shoes, or in the living room to keep cozy throws close to hand. For another option, consider a coat stand, which makes a great alternative to standard hooks on the back of the door and can be put to good use for storing towels and dressing gowns.

ABOVE **Ladder store**
Solid wood furniture and accessories can work well in a bathroom, but painting them with a moisture-resistant bathroom paint, like this ladder has been, may help them stand up to the high moisture levels in a bathroom.

LEFT Handy hanging

A hook has been well utilized here to hang a laundry bag, freeing up valuable floor space.

Wall-mounted shelving is a great way to squeeze extra space out of your bathroom, and can work in the tightest of nooks. Placed high on the wall, or above the top of a doorframe, it makes clever use of otherwise redundant space. Get organized and line the shelf with labeled boxes, baskets, or toiletry bags to store all your travel and grooming products, or use it for extra display space. The bathroom, seen opposite, rather ingeniously doubles up as a home library, making brilliant use of the dead space above the cistern. While not advisable in a main bathroom due to condensation, if the toilet is housed separately, there are no such practical limitations on what can go here.

Don't forget the small accents too: decant liquid soap and toiletries into attractive bottles, so you don't mind them being out on show, and keep them organized in a metal bottle rack or holder. Use vintage teacups or pretty bowls to keep cotton wool buds and bath salts to hand. A hanging fruit basket could make a clever home for products or even children's bath toys when floor and wall space is limited, and can be hung from a shower curtain pole. Wall-mounted wicker baskets can do a similar job to shelves in a more interesting way, holding spare towels and accessories.

If you don't have space for a sink and are planning to refit the room, a dual flush toilet (seen opposite) is well worth considering. It pushes clean water through the sink taps and recycles it into the tank below, ready to be used in the next flush. It will not only save space, but also packs great eco credentials to boot.

MAKE YOUR OWN

A riot of artwork and objets, this tiny bathroom certainly provides light entertainment for those visiting it. To make your own similar fitted shelves, take some wood (at least $\frac{1}{2}$ in (12 mm) thick is advisable for book storage) and cut it to the length of your alcove (or purchase the wood from a DIY store that will do the cutting for you). Using a wood saw, cut some wooden battens to the same width as your alcove, then cut shorter pieces to the depth of the shelf's sides, shortening them slightly to allow space for the back batten. Hold the battens in place and mark their positions onto the wall while using a spirit level to check for straightness. Drill two holes wide enough to accommodate an appropriate countersink screw, using a wood bit, into each batten; depending on the length of the battens, the holes should be around 8 in  (20 cm) from either end. Add an extra hole in the middle for longer battens. Use a countersink bit to create a depression to fit the screw head, then fix to the wall using a masonry drill bit and appropriate screw anchors (wall plugs) if required. Rest the shelves on top of the battens and secure them with wood screws, fixed through the bottom of each batten. For an extra slice of pattern, these shelf fronts were decorated with vintage postal stickers. Patterned ribbon, stuck on with double-sided tape, would also work well.

Chapter Four

CREATIVE WORKSPACES

Thanks to the online revolution, more of us than ever find ourselves working from home, whether as a remote or flexible worker for an understanding employer, or as a pioneering freelancer, carving out our own niche in the world. And with a resurgence in the popularity of craft, we have been flocking to take up sewing, knitting, and generally making our own. But a separate room dedicated to these tasks can often be an unattainable luxury, and instead this space is often required to coexist within another room. Whether you use a HOME OFFICE to run your business, write a blog, or simply keep on top of the bills, or a CRAFT ROOM as part of your professional work or as a hobby, an environment that works for you can be created in the most modest of spaces and help your work or hobby fit in with your home and lifestyle.

Block painted mini canvases look sweet floating above a desk area and are easy to create yourself

HOME OFFICES
Setting up shop in style

When setting up your workplace from home, first think about the practical considerations and what, if anything, you need to buy. Do you need a dedicated desk space for a computer, or can you operate from a laptop at the sofa or dining table? (Will you be disciplined enough to concentrate on business tasks if you're not in a designated work zone?) Could you get a wireless printer, enabling you to tuck it away out of sight in a cupboard without needing to be tethered to it? Are there power points available near your work area? Do you need to be able to clear everything away with ease at the end of each day to make way for homework or family dinners?

If you don't already have a desk, rather than visiting an office supplies store to purchase a bland faux-wood variety, often so ubiquitous in the modern workplace, think about what else might work in its place. Could you balance an old door on top of some trestle legs, or stacks of breeze blocks, and top it with glass, for an inexpensive take on the industrial look? Or set up your workspace on a drop-leaf table, easily folding it away when not in use? You could even customize your chosen table by creating a freestanding raised shelf to sit your monitor on, providing shallow space underneath to stow away the keyboard. Try gluing two wooden battens at either end of a narrow piece of wood, cut to the same depth, and simply placing it on your desk. If your desktop area is small, see if you can tuck items like a printer underneath it on a small stool to keep things clutter-free.

If you spend most of your working days sitting at your home computer, it's worth investing in a proper computer chair. Their aesthetic can often leave a lot to be desired, however, so scour the web for online retailers selling less corporate-looking designs. If your search draws a blank, consider buying a design that will serve you well on a practical level, then disguise it to feel more in-keeping with your style by adding a cushion pad in a fabric you love and draping it with nice throws, or even make a bespoke semi-fitted cover for it. If it's more of a part-time perch, however, then you needn't worry so much: look out for old kitchen chairs, stools, or even a tall pouffe, which can double as extra guest seating when you're socializing rather than working.

MAKE YOUR OWN

Storage that marries practical and display can only ever be a good thing. Here, a set of customized wire coat hangers enables this graphic designer to keep current magazines, referenced for work, close at hand. This would also work well as an alternative to a night (bedside) table in a small space, to store current reads. To create a chain of several hangers, take some pliers, place the head of the second hanger halfway along the bottom bar of the first hanger, and simply bend and twist the head around it to secure into place. Repeat the process as many times as you like, though bear in mind that the longer it gets, the heavier it will become when magazines are hanging on it, so you may need to consider the wall fixing it is resting on. Leave plain or, for a more decorative look, add on a few stripes of colored masking tape, or wrap the entire piece with ribbon or wool for a more crafty aesthetic.

LEFT Bright and bijou

A wall-mounted cubby unit provides handy access to stationery, as well as giving something pretty to look at, especially when painted in a cheery, bright hue. Look out for old drinks crates to create something similar at home.

BELOW Tidy table

An old hall table provides a perfect spot for a laptop when temporary desk space is required. A classic Anglepoise is an ideal task lamp for a workspace, with the bonus of still looking stylish once the laptop is packed away.

Storage is key within a home office, arguably more so than anywhere else in the house, particularly to aid any admin or to store any work paraphernalia related to your business. If this can be done seamlessly, it will enable you to spend more time on the more enjoyable aspects of your work and less time chasing your tail. Whether your office is simply a section of another space or housed in a dedicated spare room at home, embrace the stylistic freedom that working on your own terms can provide and keep its aesthetic in line with the rest of your home, rather than recreating another soulless office-cubicle-style space. Bring as many non-office elements into its design as you can, while keeping the set-up practical and organized. Storage cubbyholes can be used to mix up both useful and decorative items, and are handy for holding smaller paraphernalia, such as paper clips, rubber bands, USB sticks, and stamps. Store practical items in pretty small bowls or containers, and look out for vintage stationery cans in thrift stores to decant your new supplies into. Cover ring binders in decorative sheets of craft or wrapping paper, and use wooden magazine racks to store paperwork in order, painting the fronts in favorite colors or simply sticking postcards over them for added interest.

If you don't like your office being out on show but don't have a dedicated room to keep it in, then a piece of furniture that can hide it away could offer the perfect solution. This clever mid-century unit, despite being designed long before the era of the home computer, makes an excellent workspace for a laptop or for simply writing or drawing. With cubbyholes in its doors, wide drawers at the bottom, and alcoves to store pens and stationery at the back, it can hold a huge amount of stuff in a very compact space. And the best part is, when folded away, no one would be any the wiser that it was there. Visiting flea markets and scouring auction sites online might well unearth something along these lines, but you could also adapt another item of furniture for use in a similar way. An old writing bureau, or even a vintage kitchen dresser with a fold-down worktop in the middle, are two such pieces that could be put to this use: their fold-down fronts can just as well hold a laptop as a notepad, and you may even find a design that could accommodate a flat-screen monitor, when pushed toward the back. Alternatively, consider converting an old wardrobe into a hideaway home office: install some shelves to provide a place for your computer and storage for files and stationery, with space at the bottom for a printer and scanner. You could even leave a gap to accommodate an office stool underneath the monitor shelf, ensuring the entire set-up can be shut totally away when not in use. Attach some corkboard to the inside doors for a handy place to store notes and favorite tearsheets or postcards.

ABOVE **Now you see it...**
The styling on top of this hidden desk unit helps it to feel even more like an innocuous cupboard when the doors are closed. The lamp on top provides both ambient room light and useful task light when you are working.

RIGHT
Monochrome storage
This tiny corner of a home office or craft room is packed with storage, thanks to these large industrial drawer units, wall-mounted medicine cabinets, and the old boxes and cases stacked on top of both of them.

A vintage crate makes a good printer table, with space inside it for storing paper.

When incorporating a workspace into a room with another use, setting it up in a natural alcove, recess, or even under a stairwell makes an economical use of space, without encroaching too much into the remainder of the room. Ensuring its styling and décor is in keeping with its surroundings can help it disappear even more. The fitted shelves above this desk on the left, made from old scaffolding planks, have been used in every other room of this home too, and as such feel very much a part of the space. The charming vintage table housing this home office (see opposite), which belongs to owners of an upcycling furniture business, showcases their signature style and fits in with the many other restored and customized pieces that appear throughout their home. While a window view at work can be lovely, if you require extra privacy, fixing up a café-style half-height curtain can help to zone off the space (as well as hiding your computer from outside view): this one is held in place by simply pegging the fabric to a curtain wire. Alternatively, you may wish to try to define the space, to separate it visually from the rest of the room. Color is a brilliant way to do this. Either paint the walls and furniture where your office area is set up in a complementary yet contrasting hue, or use different colored art and accessories. If space allows, you might wish to create a physical divide in the room by setting up an open shelving unit, or you could use a freestanding screen to denote the office area.

ABOVE **Room to read**
Tucked into a corner of the living room, this desk creates a nook to catch up on paperwork, while still being a part of this social room.

OPPOSITE **Vintage office**
The clear Perspex "ghost" chair used at this desk adds a contemporary twist to this predominantly vintage scheme, and is softened with a sheepskin rug. Honeycomb paper balls create a touch of fun in the corner, and are lightweight enough to be taped to the ceiling.

RIGHT **Up in the eaves**
A cozy, light-filled spot in the eaves of this live/work studio makes an ideal space to tuck an office, where its limited head height would make it unsuitable as a main living area.

DECORATIVE *Pinboard*

Reuse a spare picture frame to create a bespoke pinboard that's both pretty and practical. This project is also a great way to utilize an old frame with missing glass. Keep an eye out in thrift or charity shops for a bargain.

Extra Ideas

• Upgrade an existing pinboard by wrapping it in fabric, pulling it taut, and fixing it in place with some duct tape at the back, making it easy to remove if the pinboard belongs to your landlord.

• Take a sheet of scrap wood and paint it with magnetic chalkboard paint. You will be able to write on it directly, as well as use magnets to hold loose papers in place on its surface. Lean it against the wall as an option to hanging, if necessary.

• Hang a length of twine around two nails above your desk and attach mini clothespins to it to provide a spot for notes and favorite postcards. If nailing isn't an option, use adhesive putty (Blu-Tack) to fix the clothespins directly to the wall temporarily.

You Will Need:

An old picture frame

Spraypaint, if required (see step 2)

Several sheets of thick craft paper, as large as the inside of the frame

Pencil

Scissors

Decorative-headed pins

1. If the old picture frame still has its glass in, remove this, along with its backing board.

2. You may wish to spraypaint your frame before continuing—if so, give it a good clean with some warm soapy water first, then let dry. Lay down an old sheet outside, place the frame in the middle, then evenly spraypaint it all over, covering the inner and outer edges, building up the color in several layers. Let dry.

3. Meanwhile, lay the backing board from the frame on top of one of the sheets of the craft paper, to use as a template. Draw round it with a pencil, then cut out. Repeat with the remaining sheets of paper.

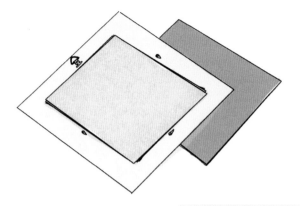

4. Take your frame and place it face down, then insert each sheet of craft paper, one on top of the other, where the glass would have been. (By using several sheets, you will provide some natural cushioning to create the pinboard effect.) Place the wooden backing board over these and fix into position.

5. Hang the frame on your wall, using the existing fixings on the back of the frame. As the frame will now be quite light, since it no longer contains the glass, a simple nail or picture hook should be enough to support it.

6. Use the decorative-headed pins to fix items to the board, pushing them down at an angle to pierce through the paper itself, rather than straight toward the back.

Make the most of your walls when surface space is at a premium by learning to make your own hanging planters on page 170

Thanks to the Internet, it's easier than ever to set up a craft business from home. From sites like Etsy, which allows users to set up their own virtual shop within its online storefront, to the ever-growing number of website-building services making it easy for anyone to build their own online store, the proliferation of craft businesses is now greater than ever. Creating room to work in can be tricky when space is at a premium, but forward planning will help alleviate this. By making your craft room as visually appealing as possible, it will become a place in which you want to spend time, and with clever organization you can increase your productivity, too.

A drop-leaf table, like the one shown, is invaluable in this set-up, where the space has to work as both a home office and a craft space. By keeping it relatively uncluttered, it's easy to accommodate both purposes and adjust the table size to suit the task at hand. Try to store your craft items in such a way that you can easily pack up and transport them as your storage needs change; or arrange them stylishly and close to hand, like the fabrics stacked on this textile designer's bookshelf. Think of your work kit as both decoration and inspiration, prompting your creativity at a glance.

CRAFT ROOMS
Allowing your imagination to run wild

Carve out space for crafting where you can. Here, a wider-than-average landing makes for a brilliant impromptu craft area for all the family to enjoy, with every available bit of space being put to good use. Despite being full of handcrafted touches, it still manages to feel like a part of the rest of the house, in part thanks to stylish storage.

One integral part of many creative spaces is a moodboard or inspiration wall. Whether used to place current work projects, inspirational tearsheets, or simply things that reflect your personal taste, it's a go-to place for inspiration at a glance when you suffer a creative dip. A basic pinboard is an adequate background, but to make it as creative as its contents, try wrapping it in fabric, secured at the back with tape, to tie the look together.

Alternatively, a series of clipboards attached to your wall creates a more structured arrangement, perfect for organizing individual projects or separating different ideas. Cover the clipboards in pretty papers or paint them in bright colors. Seek out the unusual: try wrapping some chicken wire around an old empty frame, or even leaning an old shutter against the wall as somewhere to clip visuals.

Now that you have inspirational images pinned to your walls, make sure you carry on the clever streak into your craft supply storage, and try out some different ideas, tailored to suit your particular craft pursuits. A wall-mounted plate rack, for example, could be put to use to organize decorative craft papers. Slim shelving or even picture ledges could be handy spots on which to line up cotton reels or craft tapes, organized by color so you can easily find what you need. More commonly seen as a shop fitting, a pegboard can add a utilitarian edge to the home craft room and provide a place for everyday work tools, hung from simple wire hooks or pegs.

ABOVE **Frame the vision**
A large, empty frame helps visually to contain pinboard images, stopping them feeling disparate. The eclectic board within it, containing both images and small 3D objects, and held in place with decorated pins and colorful decorative masking (Washi) tape, looks striking.

RIGHT **Craft corner**
An old curtain hides a less-than-lovely table, as well as allowing for a sewing machine (and unfinished craft projects) to be hidden underneath it.

ABOVE LEFT Desk detail

A kitsch desk display adds humor to a workspace. This punched-metal plant pot has been repurposed and now keeps everyday items to hand, whilst decorative masking tape and twine look pretty when left out on display.

ABOVE MIDDLE Pretty papers

Rolls of fabric and giftwrap are cleverly stored out on show in this repurposed wicker bottle carrier, which is easy to move elsewhere if required, thanks to its carry handle.

ABOVE RIGHT Craft supply storage

Old jars and food cans are put to good use holding a selection of crafting supplies. A pretty crochet trim, attached with double-sided tape, makes a feature of this otherwise plain shelf front.

LEFT Crate arrangement

Wine crates can provide great informal storage. They are easy to stack on the floor and you can add or remove them to suit your needs. Customize, if you like, by covering them with decorative paper.

MAKE YOUR OWN

Not everything looks lovely out on show, however, and a certain amount of hidden storage is always advisable. Cupboards are invaluable for hiding the less aesthetically pleasing kit you'd rather not have on public view. This customized cupboard has been treated to a makeover, to help it fit in perfectly with the rest of the crafty space it resides in. To create something similar at home, first give your cupboard door a good clean and remove its handle. Gather together a selection of patterned papers — wallpaper, giftwrap, art papers, or even book pages would work, as long as the paper's not too thin. Cut into small squares of equal size, using a guillotine or a ruler and craft knife. Prepare some white craft glue in an old pot,

watering it down if it's very thick; then, one at a time, dip each cut square into the glue so that it coats both sides. Wipe off the excess glue on the side of the bowl and stick the square into place on the cabinet. Repeat until the whole door is covered, pressing excess paper over the edges of the door for a neat look. Let dry, then coat with a couple more layers of the glue mix, for an extra hardwearing finish.

Often in a creative space, it can be hard to tell where the decorative ends and the practical begins, so aim to employ that approach in your own craft area. Look beyond purpose-made storage boxes and turn to the kitchen, bathroom, or even outside space for containers and solutions that will work here, too. Spice jars could work wonderfully as storage for beadworking items, whilst tankards, cans, and old shop baskets could easily be used to contain paintbrushes, sewing pins, or rolls of yarn. It's not about perfection or obsessed-over arrangements; it's about simply embracing the relatively everyday things we have around us in a more decorative way.

ABOVE **Crafter's delight**
A dedicated sewing desk is many crafters' dream, and a raised shelf and a peg rail above it helps to keep the countertop clear. A row of bulldog clips fastened to a strip of wood allows for an ever-changing display space, as well as keeping things close to hand.

ABOVE Tower of tins

In addition to looking charming, old tins can help to keep small items organized in a workplace. Add chalkboard labels to their fronts to keep track of what's where, or implement a color-coding system, assigning different item types to different colored tins.

ABOVE MIDDLE Project parts

A current craft project is stored safely and out of the way in this small saucer, ready to be returned to later.

ABOVE RIGHT Working décor

See the things around you in a new light: these working artist's palettes are hung on the wall when not in use, creating some instant art in their own right. Non-painters can look out for similar at antiques fairs.

RIGHT Grand illusion

The basic windows of this shed are aesthetically elevated, thanks to some salvaged stained glass panels being leant over them.

BELOW Bags of storage

An old enamel table is a practical choice for any messy work since it can be easily cleaned, and you can use it to work on a laptop or tablet. Clutter is hidden by stringing a curtain under the tabletop. Shelving, for both storage and display, is made from offcuts of wood and fitted on metal brackets. Painting the walls helps to lighten and lift the space. Even the rafters have been put to work here, as storage for art canvases.

If you're crying out for additional workspace but an extension isn't on the cards, a humble garden shed could provide the perfect solution. As long as you have some form of outdoor space, a shed-workroom can offer valuable extra room for homeowners and renters alike. Even the most humble of sheds can be put to some form of work use: the key is good ventilation. Ensure the base of your shed is raised from the ground and that, while it's watertight, there is still good air circulation. Think about the positioning of the shed: if possible, site it close to the house or directly off a pathway so you don't have to cross a muddy lawn to get to your desk space. Run an electric heater in there during cooler months to keep you cozy and reduce moisture levels in the air, helping to combat any damp. Unless you plan on taking your set-up a step further and fully insulating and draught-proofing the shed, it's advisable not to keep any electronic equipment or valuables out there full-time: instead, just bring them out when you need to work. If you aren't able to install power directly in the shed itself, run an extension cable from the house, which can power laptops and lamps. For safety, plug it into an earth leakage circuit breaker (ELCB) socket indoors. Revel in having an extra informal space to decorate by throwing caution to the wind and indulging in a little fantasy styling: the artist owner of this shed workspace regularly alters the ambience with a change of theme, as seen here in the touches of Wild West styling.

RIGHT Secret office

Painted a delicate off-white, this shed feels more like an extension of the house rather than an off-the-shelf garden shed. A wall-mounted vintage garden tool helps it blend into its surroundings.

Hooks fixed to the back of the door are useful for both art aprons and gardening tools

CRAFT SUPPLIES *Storage Rack*

Keep your craft kit at hand without cluttering your desk by using some lateral thinking to create this useful storage rack. For a uniform look, use cans of the same size throughout, or mix things up to accommodate your various items in different-sized cans, as needed.

You Will Need:

Wire grid (see step 1 for guidance)

Spraypaint, if required (see step 2)

Old food cans, cleaned and labels removed

Tape measure

Ruler

Pencil

Scissors

Decorative papers—such as craft paper, wallpaper or wrapping paper—enough to cover the cans

Double-sided tape

Bias binding

Electric drill with metal drill bit suitable for making a pilot hole

Wire and wire cutters

Screws and screw anchors (wall plugs) appropriate for your wall type

Renter's Alternatives

● Create a mini version of this by hanging two or three cans from a single nail in the wall, suspending them on string or ribbon instead of wire at different heights.

● If you have a magnetic board (or even a filing cabinet) in your workspace, glue some magnets to the back of each can and stick them straight onto that instead.

● If hanging from the wall isn't an option, create several cans for your desk but keep things organized by ensuring each one is a different height, so it's easier to differentiate between them. Fix them together with more double-sided tape to make one self-contained item.

1. For this project you will need to find a grid of some kind, such as an old wire headboard from a child's bed, a wire display grid, a piece of wooden trellis, or even an old wire cooling rack. If it is not new, give your grid a good clean.

2. You may wish to spraypaint your frame before continuing—if so, give it a good clean with some warm soapy water first, then let dry. Lay down an old sheet outside, place the frame in the middle, then evenly spraypaint it all over, covering the inner and outer edges, building up the color in several layers. Let dry.

3. Measure the height and circumference of one of your cans. On a sheet of decorative paper, draw on this measurement, allowing a ¾in (2 cm) excess on the circumference, and cut out the rectangle. Repeat until you have enough paper shapes to cover all your cans, altering the measurements if/as necessary.

4. Run a length of double-sided tape around the top and bottom of each can, then, taking your first piece of paper, stick this neatly around the can, following along its edges. Apply an extra strip of double-sided tape down the excess length along the back, then stick this down.

5. To neaten off the top of the can and hide any sharp edges, cover with a strip of bias binding cut to the same length as the can's

circumference, and stick strips of double-sided tape along both edges of the binding's underside. Remove the protective strip from the tape and stick the binding into place, with one half on the inside and one on the outside of the can. Repeat steps 4 and 5 with the other cans.

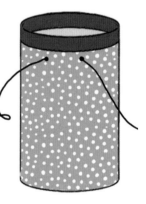

7. Feed one of the lengths of wire through the first hole then back out again until both protruding ends are the same length, creating a small loop inside the can. Twist the two wire ends a few times so that they are tight against the outside of the can, then twist them around the frame. Repeat with the other cans.

6. Once all the cans are complete, drill two small holes in the back of each one, a thumb's width down from the top of the can and about two thumbs' widths apart from each other, using your electric drill and drill bit and holding the can tight in your other hand.

8. Fix your wire frame to the wall: if it's not too big and heavy, a couple of nails might hold it, otherwise fix a couple of screws into the wall for the frame to sit on. Ensure you use the right screws and screw anchors (wall plugs) for your wall type before drilling.

Chapter Five

PLANTS AND OUTDOOR LIVING

Greenery adds, quite literally, life and vitality to any space, and should be considered an essential element of your home both inside and out, however small or modest the gesture. After falling somewhat out of fashion in recent years, humble house PLANTS are now being embraced by homeowners more than ever, partly due our increasingly cramped city living spaces, meaning we have less connection to the Great Outdoors. Though if you're lucky enough to have any OUTDOOR LIVING space, you may be reluctant to get green-fingered if it's not your property or you're likely to move on before any plants have fully grown. By treating the space like any other within the home, and using styling tricks rather than costly planting to add personality, you can create a look that's all your own, from a sprawling patch of countryside to the tiniest urban oasis.

The abundance of green plants in this window works perfectly with the green sofa and wicker chairs

PLANTS
Adding life to your interior

House plants are a great way to add delicate texture, lush greenery, and splashes of life to your living space, and it doesn't take too much of a green finger to create a modest and charming collection of plants in the home. A simple display, however basic or common the plants may be, can have a surprising impact on how a room feels, especially when grouped en masse at staggered heights, as seen opposite.

While DIY stores and supermarkets have a wide selection of plants on offer, many of us will have experienced buying a cheap variety we know nothing about as an impulse buy, then watching it slowly die in a corner while we wonder what we're doing wrong. Buck the trend and try making a concerted effort to go further afield to a dedicated nursery or garden center, to make the most of their free expert advice and greater offerings, ensuring you are investing your efforts wisely.

Selecting pots can be just as important as choosing the plant itself, both practically and aesthetically. While the temptation can be simply to leave it in its original plastic pot, most plants would benefit from repotting into something a little larger at this stage, to allow for extra growth. Ceramic or plastic pots work equally well, as long as the plant has adequate drainage. If you aren't double potting—retaining an inner pot with drainage holes—ensure your chosen pot has drainage holes in its bottom, and sit it on a saucer to protect surfaces. Plastic pots can be considerably cheaper than ceramic ones, but can look it, too. However, both are easy to personalize to match your interior: spraypaint, paper decoupage (see page 153 for advice on this technique), or simply wrapping in fabric can create an excellent disguise for a less-than-pretty pot. Topping the dirt with decorative pebbles or even shells can help it to feel like a considered part of an interior, and will also hide its inner plastic pot, if it has one, creating a more seamless look.

BELOW
Grow your own
Keep growing vegetables
and herbs in a trug in the
kitchen so they're easy to
move aside if extra
workspace is needed.

A lack of garden needn't stop you creating your own small-scale plot for growing herbs and vegetables. If you have a warm, sunny area by a window in your kitchen or dining room, you can easily set something up here, with the added bonus of ensuring your produce will be close to hand when cooking. To maximize the success of your crop, do your research and stick to varieties that are more likely to do well both indoors, and with the light levels available to them. Growing from seed can be by far the cheapest way to get started, but to keep costs lower still, consider holding a seed swap with friends so you can spread the

variety out without having to buy too many packets individually. Sprinkle seeds into a seed tray filled with seed-sewing soil mix (compost), or if there's no space to dedicate to a whole tray, set up a DIY version along a narrow windowsill. To do so, cut some toilet rolls in half, then make several evenly spaced snips about ½ in (1 cm) into the bottom of each one, before bending them over to create a base. Then fill with the same soil mix and seeds. If space allows, starting seedlings off in an indoor mini greenhouse or terrarium will help to keep them warm and regulate their temperature, as well as looking decorative.

When they are big enough to be planted, transfer them to individual larger pots, or set up a single large container to hold multiple plants, such as an old crate lined with plastic (make sure you add drainage holes underneath and place on a tray to catch drips). During the different seasons, you'll learn what works well in your home environment through the process of trial and error. If you don't have space for a dedicated plant-growing area, try to incorporate them as part of your décor by planting in attractive containers and using them in place of houseplants or flowers, ensuring they remain in a sunny spot like a tabletop situated by a window.

If growing from seed sounds like too much hard work for you, consider starting up with decorative succulents, including cacti. Renowned for being easy to care for due to their tolerance of drought, they are perfect for the neglectful gardener because they can, for the most part, be left to their own devices. They come in a bewildering array of colors and varieties, so check the guidance label on any plants before purchasing them to ensure that this particular variety will thrive within its chosen environment. As a rule, green varieties can often be hardier than colored ones, and most succulents thrive in direct sunlight, so if you're looking for something to go in a shady corner, a fern or evergreen might be a better choice. Possibly the easiest option of all, however, is the air plant. This unusual, exotic breed does not require soil to survive: it simply needs a container (use your imagination) and occasional watering.

ABOVE TOP **Kitsch and cute**
Scour thrift stores for unusual planters, like this cute donkey design. Flank a statement piece such as this one with a selection of plain pots, allowing it to steal the show.

ABOVE **Potted pretties**
The delicate balance of succulents mixed with *objets* in this artist's workspace creates an almost painterly feel in its own right.

Up on a ledge
A small corner shelf, fixed high up on the wall, is a simple yet effective perch for this beautiful cascading plant, and helps to soften the look of this dining area.

Trailing and hanging plants can be an obvious solution for space-strapped homes, freeing up precious surface areas, as well as adding a bold splash of texture and greenery, which serves as an added bonus if you're not able to paint or decorate your space otherwise. Indoor hanging baskets are the easiest way to suspend a plant, but if you don't want to (or can't) attach a hanging hook in your ceiling to support one, hang the pots from curtain poles, picture rails, or the sides of furniture instead, using an S-hook to secure them. Placing potted plants high up on a piece of furniture that would otherwise be redundant will also achieve a similar effect, allowing the plant to trail downwards. Ensure you are still able to access any awkwardly placed plants, to give them water and plant food, if required, or stick to plant types that don't need regular watering, for ease.

An upside-down planter could also be an interesting modern alternative to a traditional hanging basket planter. Its specially designed pot, which allows you to hang plants the wrong way up, has the bonus of aiding the plants' water conservation through a special reservoir system, and as such can be a good option for notoriously tricky plants such as orchids. For a more vintage-style look, track down an old wire birdcage, which can prove a novel home for potted plants, with space between its bars through which trailing plants can hang. Clear glass hanging terrariums, in contrast, can provide an almost futuristic look.

ABOVE **Go green**
Set against a backdrop of green tiles, the mixture of foliage and flowers on this fireplace helps it feel alive.

MAKE YOUR OWN

Miniature paper bunting is quick and easy to rustle up, and can be a good use for old scraps of decorative paper, music pages, or even old maps. With a slightly more graphic feel than traditional fabric bunting, it frames this window to perfection while picking up on the colored bottles on the shelf below. Create a perfectly even bunting template by folding a small rectangular scrap sheet of paper in half lengthwise, then lay it down and use your ruler to draw a straight line from the corner of the folded edge at the bottom to the outer edge at the top. Cut along the line, then fold open ready for use. When you have enough triangles, take your twine, around 16 in (40 cm) longer than the length of the area you wish to hang the bunting in, then around 8 in (20 cm) from one end, fold over the top of a triangle by around ¹⁄₂ in (1 cm), placing the twine in the fold. Run a glue stick over the short flap, then stick it to the triangle, pressing firmly. When it is dry, cut off the protruding underside of the flap to leave you with a neat triangle shape. Repeat along the length of your twine, allowing a short even space in between each triangle, and ensuring you have around 8 in (20 cm) excess twine at the other end too, to allow for fixings.

TOP
BOTTOM

LEFT **Strikingly sculptural**

Twigs, picked up on a country walk, look architectural when placed in a tall vase.

BELOW **Floral specimens**

Old lab jars, test tubes, and flasks can lend an eccentric feel to a tabletop floral display, and suit a more utilitarian interiors scheme.

Nothing quite lights up a room like a beautiful bunch of fresh flowers, but regular trips to the florist for their finest bouquets is a luxury not many of us can afford. Instead, embrace the creative challenge and beauty of a simpler arrangement, and make the most of what you have to hand. Single stems, when spread between vessels, can make a striking statement and lend a modern touch to a room. Supermarkets can be a great place to buy bargain seasonal blooms, but, if you are able, try a zero-cost approach and take cuttings of flowers, wildflowers, and plants from a garden space instead. Even if the plant or flower itself isn't exceptional, by employing a well-curated blend of cuttings and containers you can still create a stunning focal point. Mix and match different flowers and greenery for a casual country look, or use long, single lengths of foliage and twigs to form a more structural display. Anything able to hold water can be used to display your blooms, so use your imagination and see what you already have at home: jam jars, tea caddies, old perfume bottles, and pretty iced tea bottles can all be used to create a stunning centerpiece, particularly when grouped en masse.

HANGING *Plantpot Holder*

A simplified version of the classic 1970s macramé plant pot holder, this project is perfect for people who are pushed for surface space.

You Will Need:

27–40 ft (8–12 m) colored cotton twine

Scissors

A plantpot or bowl slightly larger than your plant base (choose one without drainage holes)

A small amount of gravel

A small plant (a cactus or succulent is ideal, because it won't grow drastically)

Superglue (optional)

1. Cut eight lengths of twine, each one about 40–60 in (100–150 cm) long. (The longer they are, the longer your finished planter will be.) Lay them out evenly together, then gather them all up at one end and tie into one big knot, leaving around 4 in (10 cm) of twine trailing from below the knot.

2. Rest the rope on a tabletop, then create a cross shape with the longer lengths of twine, with each section containing two strands of the twine.

3. Take two of these strands from the same section, and tie them together in a double knot, around two thumb widths higher than the base knot. Repeat with the three other sections.

4. Separate the strands back out, then take the right-hand strand from one knot and pair it with the left-hand strand from the knot on its right. Knot these together too, around two thumb widths higher than your last knots. Work around the piece until all four corners are knotted, leaving you with a square shape with a cross running through the middle.

5. Repeat the same technique: take the right-hand strand from one knot and tie it together with the left-hand strand from the knot on its immediate right, tying it into a double knot about two thumb widths higher than the two existing knots. Work around the other corners doing the same thing, leaving you with a larger square shape with a diamond shape in the middle.

6. Sprinkle a thin layer of gravel in the bottom of your plantpot, to assist with drainage. Place your plant inside, adjusting the amount of gravel, if required, to ensure the inner pot doesn't protrude above the outer pot. Place the potted plant in the middle of your knotted square. Lift up all the lengths of twine and gather them above the center of the plant, then carefully lift the whole thing up. The plantpot should be supported by the knotted sections of the bowl, with the central knot hanging from the bottom point.

7. Decide how long you want your hanging plantpot holder to be. At this length, twist the rope to create a large loop at the top, around 4 in (10 cm) long, then tie it securely in a knot. Cut off all the excess twine. For extra strength, you may wish to squeeze in some superglue around both knots, making sure it doesn't dribble out. Hang the plant-pot holder on either a nail or a hook in your wall.

White planters look great in black plantholders made from these instructions, as part of an otherwise store-bought display

Extra Ideas

• For a more colorful finish, use brightly hued twines—you could even use multiple colors within one piece.

• Create a display space for cut flowers, too: stick to a round vase, or even something a little quirkier like a teapot, to ensure the vessel fills out the macramé, then fill with water and display your blooms

• Hang in small outdoor spaces too: seasonal potted flowers can hang from a hook on a balcony wall, the edge of a fence, or from a tree branch (see page 184 for an example of the latter).

Colorful melamine plates give a twist to the traditional interior wall lined with best china, and will not break if they are accidentally knocked down

Gardening itself is, of course, a large element of tending an outside space. But in a home-for-now, where you may not actually own the garden (or yard, or terrace), or don't feel you will be around to see the benefits of years of graft and investment in it, the approach can be somewhat different. Embrace the challenge by approaching it in much the same way you might any other room in your home: changing what you can, covering what you can't and adding your own personal touches wherever possible. Have fun experimenting—this could be the opportunity to embrace bolder design ideas, outside of your usual decorating spectrum.

A decent patch of land, however small, can be considered a luxury in many places, especially in cities. If you're renting, you may find that landlords can be less precious about their outdoor space, and may be more willing to give you free rein to adapt as you wish. Landscaping can be a costly, long-term project, so even if you do own, instead look at smaller changes you can make. Simply painting a shed in a cheery hue, tying up cheap bamboo fencing to add privacy, or graveling over a small boggy lawn are all relatively easy tasks to complete that can make a huge difference. To soften a concrete yard, consider fake grass, which is easy to lay and can literally be rolled up again when you need to move on.

Pot plants are always a great investment if you're reluctant or unable to plant straight into the ground, as they can easily be taken with you when you move on. Save money on expensive plants by growing from seed or bulbs where appropriate, or fill up the space with inexpensive seasonal bedding plants, which are only a short-term commitment. Another frugal way to build up your garden is to propagate from other plants—ask a green-fingered friend or relative to let you take some cuttings of their perennial or woody plants. Take their advice, or consult gardening books, on the best way to plant them up, because this varies from plant to plant.

OUTDOOR LIVING
Creating space out in the open

In an apartment block, private outdoor space can be a rarity, so make the most of whatever you have, whether it's a dedicated balcony or merely a spot for a few pots by your front door. The space may need to work extra-hard as somewhere to grow fresh food and herbs, cultivate plants, and provide additional sitting and dining space, while looking lovely to boot. Even a few pot plants need a modest gardening kit, so think about how you can store it successfully. A bench with under-seat storage, for example, could be the perfect stowaway for tools and seed packets, and a metal container could be used to store spare soil mix (compost), rather than having it slumped in a corner in its garish plastic sack.

In a limited space, a flexible dining set-up is a must. Opt for folding or stackable furniture you could tuck away, or even hang on wall-mounted hooks, either to free up some floor space when needed or to store safely during winter. Alternatively, consider a lightweight plastic table and chairs set for your indoor dining set-up, which can then be easily moved outdoors without risk of rain damage. If you're keen on barbecues, a space-saving one in a cheery bucket design provides an ample cooking surface for two and still looks decorative when not in use.

ABOVE **Foodies' paradise**
Keen cooks with limited outdoor space could consider an edible balcony, such as this one, crammed with herbs and vegetables. Hanging extra pots around the balcony posts maximizes the space even further.

RIGHT **Sheltered zone**
Broken old deckchairs create an innovative windbreaker for a breezy top-floor balcony. Grouping pot plants at either end of the space adds visual impact, as well as giving the plants mutual protection due to their close proximity, leaving the central area free for a table and chairs.

OPPOSITE **Party spot**
The smallest of spaces can still be welcoming with an injection of colorful accessories and personal touches, such as a shawl used to add instant color to a small table, the quirky bug stickers "crawling" over plain metal planters.

Spraypainted tin cans, tethered to balcony railings, make playful containers for cut flowers and candles

Making the most of your outdoor space needn't take much money, and can be an ongoing project, to spend time on as and when you can. Often considered something of a luxury, and certainly not what you'd expect to find in a home-for-now, an outdoor kitchen can actually be a hugely useful garden addition that significantly opens up your living and socializing space during warmer months, as well as adding real character to a garden. A similar effect can be achieved even on a shoestring budget, like the one opposite. Here, inexpensive metal shelving, primarily intended for use in a garage or basement, stands up to all weathers and offers utilitarian-style flexible shelving for storage and display, alongside a freestanding stainless-steel table, put to use as a countertop with storage space beneath. An old oven, powered by a gas cylinder, provides an alternative to the barbecue, while a simple wire grid, fixed to an external wall, is used for hanging cups and ornaments on S-hooks. Topped off with a simple garden sail for protection from the elements, this charming outdoor room offers a useful addition to the main living space, yet could easily be removed and relocated as and when required.

ABOVE AND RIGHT
Garden picnic

Set up an impromptu dining area in a communal garden space by utilizing an upturned crate as a table, to create your own posh picnic. Assemble a "picnic to go" kit to keep ready for grabbing whenever the sun comes out. Store everything you need inside your crate "table."

RIGHT Drawer substitute

An empty food can, used to store cutlery, fits perfectly with the style of this space and is a great way to reuse something otherwise destined for the trash can or recycling bin.

FAR RIGHT Hanging storage

A grid system like this could be put to use hanging all manner of cooking implements, pots, and pans, and is a flexible option for an ever-changing area.

BELOW Al fresco cooking

Mismatched styling in this clever cooking space is as much a necessity as a style choice, allowing elements to be added and amended as the space evolves.

BELOW Secret hideaway

The smallest of outdoor nooks can be given a cozy, intimate feel with a well-laid table, such as this one, tucked away at the bottom of the garden.

LEFT Layer it up

If you enjoy collecting vintage linens, don't worry about seeking out a single piece big enough to cover your tabletop. Instead, layer up several mismatched pieces to create a patchwork effect. A sturdy vintage jar works well as a casual vase, and won't be likely to get knocked over by a strong gust of wind. Pick a small posy of flowers from the garden to add extra color to your al fresco table.

Specially designed outdoor furniture can be surprisingly costly, but splashing out isn't necessarily the way to create an enticing garden space: invest time instead in the touches of individuality that you bring to it. A pub-style wooden bench is often by far the cheapest offering in DIY stores for seating six or more people, and can be painted in an array of colors, or even stripes, to personalize it. Metal tables and chairs can be a good budget choice, too, and powder-coated versions in bright hues will cheer up the smallest of spaces. Alternatively, looking in thrift stores for older pieces will aid a vintage look, with any rust spots serving to add patina and character. If you don't have space for one large table but like to host outdoor parties, collect a few old glass and metal side tables, to stand against fences or next to a barbecue, to provide additional surface space for plates or a buffet.

While wooden outdoor furniture is normally constructed of teak or hardwood, that doesn't rule out other woods altogether. Old doors are often discarded during house renovations and piled up in dumpsters and skips, yet they can make brilliant outdoor tables when placed on a couple of trestle legs. Keep an eye out in your neighborhood, too, for discarded single wooden chairs, and slowly build a collection for a casual, mismatched look. Give these wooden pieces a fighting chance of outdoor survival by coating them in hardwearing exterior wood varnish or paint, for protection, and cover them in winter with a waterproof cover if you don't have a shed or inside space to store them in. While they may not last you for decades, if you've procured them for free, the odd bit of wear and tear is easily overlooked and you can "upgrade" with new street finds as things become damaged. Revel in the eccentricity of this approach—or, if it all feels a bit much, create some visual unity by adding tablecloths and seat pads in matching or coordinating fabrics.

ABOVE
Utilize nature

Don't waste money on tablecloth weights: a small stone wrapped in colored twine makes a charming (and free) weight. Attach to upside-down metal curtain pincers, spacing them around the bottom of your tablecloth.

RIGHT
Lace makeover

Spraypaint and lace have transformed this plain white sheet of plastic into a pretty, wipe-clean tablecloth. Create your own by cutting some plastic to size, laying excess plastic around its edges to protect outdoor flooring, then place some old lace on top and spray through its gaps to create a reverse pattern.

In this colorful outdoor area, dressing plays as important a role as it does inside the house and as the actual gardening. The overriding scheme consists of pinks and oranges, carried through from the plants to the furnishings, which helps to hold the scheme together and is softened by an abundance of greenery. This tablecloth fabric, along with matching cushions used elsewhere, might look as though it is made of standard cotton, but is actually coated with polyurethane, making it water-resistant and therefore fine to leave outside for the summer. If you're looking for something similar but can't find any in patterns you like, consider making your own waterproof oilcloth fabric by coating heavy cotton or linen in linseed oil (look online for full tutorials).

The décor stretches beyond the tabletop, as seen in the cute outdoor solar-powered string lanterns, a cool shade of French gray on the shed, and an unusual decorative metal panel hanging on the wall. Adding a splash of color to ironware, or even a mirror frame, creates some interesting outdoor décor, and can be a great way to incorporate redundant industrial items. Look out, too, for old tin signs: hang several together to build up a feature wall, much as you would inside the home. Consider an outdoor rug to finish off the space and define the dining area. Colorful plastic designs, often woven in intricate patterns, can be inexpensive and low enough maintenance to leave outside for the summer season. If you still feel the space needs a focal point, keep an eye out for old metal fireplaces: leaning one up against the wall could give it a quirky focus.

RIGHT Happy colors
A "slice" of garden can benefit from being visually divided into defined areas, for storage, seating, and plants, as seen here in this vibrant outdoor space.

A cut-down old shower curtain makes an ingenious, and damp-proof, curtain at this shed window

Repurpose the broken

A damaged watering can is still useful in the garden as a plant pot, especially if it already has holes in the bottom!

ABOVE MIDDLE **Raise it up**

With a little DIY know-how, raised planters can be relatively cheap and easy to construct, and make a great homegrown vegetable patch.

ABOVE RIGHT **Upcycled tins**

Oversized tin cans make excellent free planters, so ask a local restaurant or takeaway to keep any used ones aside for you. Wash well, especially if they contained cooking oil, punch some drainage holes into the bottom with a hammer and nail, and then line with a shallow layer of gravel to ease drainage. A coating of spraypaint completes their transformation.

Amassing a collection of plant pots can soon become costly, but with a bit of imagination you can build this up with little to no outlay. Any form of container that can survive outdoors, and keep soil in and water out, can be used as a planter. Bear in mind that container plants will be more susceptible to the elements, and will quickly dry out on hot summer days, but with regular watering, there's no reason why many plants can't thrive in this set-up. Upcycled old wheelbarrows, birdbaths, and bowls can make innovative planters, but you will need a drill to add drainage holes in their bases to prevent the plants becoming waterlogged. Discarded butler's sinks, or even bathtubs, on the other hand, come complete with their own holes. Just ensure you lay a large stone or crock over the top before filling with dirt, to stop it getting clogged up. Colanders and old wire fruit baskets can be converted with the addition of hanging-basket linings. Old tires (tyres) make excellent planters, too, but will need some form of base to support the soil. Stretch out a bin bag inside one, pierce with a few holes, then secure the plastic in place by tucking it inside the rim of the tire and adding some gravel to hold it in place, making sure the plastic doesn't sag. To create a larger planter, simply add extra tires to build up the height.

BELOW Wall décor

A collection of old garden tools acts as authentic garden décor on this shed wall, but in a sheltered area, like a small balcony, you could store working tools in this way too, to act as both decoration and handy storage.

ABOVE Tiered planting

Gerberas, trailing lobelia, and simple daisies make great cheap-and-cheerful seasonal plants. If floor space is limited, utilize some old ladders and window boxes to take your storage up rather than out.

RIGHT Tassel trim

A string of fabric tassels makes great outdoor décor, and is a quirky alternative to bunting. It can be left outside for the whole summer to add a fun feel to the space.

FAR RIGHT Hang it up

Macramé hanging plant pots (see page 170) look beautiful hanging from a tree and could also be used along a wall or fence in a much smaller garden to maximize planting space. For a similar look, tie up a collection of empty drink bottles and fill with single cut flowers for a striking display.

BELOW Pave the way

These sweet concrete paving slabs were actually made by the owner, using silicon cake tins and flat decorative items, such as leaves and doilies, cast into their top. Simply placed on the ground, they could easily be lifted up if required.

Whatever decorating restrictions you may have in the home, the garden can often be the place to unleash your creativity and have a little more fun. It needn't be a big bold statement: build up small details to complement your surroundings and utilize nature. While you may have inherited elements you can't change, such as an overhanging tree, instead of bemoaning the shadows it casts, embrace it as part of your décor by using its branches to suspend decorative items, such as jam jars of votives (tea lights) or pretty teacups used as bird feeders, filled with seeds. Set it up as a cozy nook by creating a simple tepee underneath, using an old bedsheet and some bamboo poles, and pile with cushions, as a temporary daytime retreat. You could even wrap its trunk in strips of pretty fabric offcuts, or "yarn bomb" it by knitting it its own colorful crochet cover. Set up your own bespoke outdoor lighting by taking an old broken chandelier, removing all its electrical elements, then simply replacing the old bulb fixings with pillar candles and hanging it from a basket hook. Customize your own plant markers by painting large pebbles in bright colors before writing on the names, or create a bespoke piece of outdoor wall art by hanging up an unwanted wooden palette and painting each slat a different color. By allowing your imagination to run riot, without the confines of walls, you might find the possibilities are limitless.

MAKE YOUR OWN

Fabric strips have long been used as a thrifty craft material to create traditional rag rugs, made using clothing and bedlinen too worn for repair. Here, they come into their element by becoming the star of this pretty hanging decoration. Take some old fabric and cut into 1 in (2.5 cm) wide strips, slightly longer than you wish your finished piece to be. Source or make a circular object to act as its core (a sturdy piece of wire bent into a circle, a large metal embroidery hoop, or even the frame of an old bicycle wheel will do). Begin to tie each length of fabric to the top, working your way around, then tie on some twine at three equally spaced points on the metal hoop to form its hanging mechanism. Tie to the branch of a tree or suspend from a basket hook above a tabletop, and watch it dance in the breeze all summer long.

RECOMMENDED STORES AND RESOURCES

HOMEWARES

Cool chain stores

IKEA: The undisputed king of affordable, customizable, and modern furniture and home accessories. Avoid kitting your space out in it from head-to-toe and use pieces sparingly, mixed in with vintage pieces, for an individual look.
USA: www.ikea.com/800-434-4532
UK: www.ikea.co.uk/0845 355 1141

Anthropologie: Outstanding collection of unusual accessories and artefacts from around the globe; great for adding character to every room in the home.
USA: www.anthropologie.com/800-309-2500
UK: www.anthropologie.eu/0800 0026 8476

West Elm: Dedicated to making it easy (and affordable) to furnish and dress your home, take advantage of their free Design Lab service and book in to see a stylist at home or in-store to help redesign your space, with no minimum spend requirement.
USA: www.westelm.com/888-922-4119
UK: www.westelm.co.uk/0800 404 9780

H&M: Just like their fashion line, their home collection stocks a mix of brilliant basics and fun fashion-inspired pieces at low price points, with particularly strong bathroom accessories and bedlinen offerings.
USA: www.hm.com/855-466-7467
UK: www.hm.com/0844 736 9000

Zara Home: A striking and beautiful range—mix and match their pieces for an eclectic look.
USA: www.zarahome.com/877-550-1107
UK: www.zarahome.com/0800 026 0091

Home organization/practical

USA: **Container Store**
www.containerstore.com
800-266-8246 (check out their dedicated "dorm rooms" section for great space-saving product ideas)

UK: **A Place for Everything**
www.aplaceforeverything.co.uk
UK: **Lakeland**
www.lakeland.co.uk/01539 488100

Space-saving gadgets

Joseph Joseph: A fun range of colorful dual-purpose kitchenware perfect for small kitchens, such as salad bowls with built-in tongs and nesting-bowl sets.
USA: www.josephjoseph.com/866-940-1875
UK: www.josephjoseph.com/020 7261 1800

Lovely individual websites

USA: **Leif**, www.leifshop.com
USA: **Uncommon Goods**
www.uncommongoods.com/888-365-0056
USA: **Jayson Home**
www.jaysonhome.com/800-472-1885
UK: **Rockett St George**
www.rockettstgeorge.co.uk/01444 253391
UK: **Graham & Green**
www.grahamandgreen.co.uk/0845 130 6622
UK: **REfoundobjects**
www.re-foundobjects.com/01434 634567

Handcrafted and designer-makers

Etsy: One of the biggest websites in the world for handmade and vintage items. Anyone can set up a store for free, meaning that millions of items are offered for sale at any one time.
USA/UK: www.etsy.com (worldwide shipping available—selected items only)

Notonthehighstreet: Akin to an online arts and crafts fair, this ever-growing website sells a vast range of goods from carefully selected small businesses.
USA/UK: www.notonthehighstreet.com (worldwide shipping available—selected items only)

Home office supplies

Staples: Kit out your desk area in style to complement your existing décor.
USA: www.staples.com/800-333-3330
UK:www/staples.co.uk/0844 546 7777

USA: **Schoolhouse Electrical & Supply Co.**
www.schoolhouseelectric.com/800-630-7113
UK: **Paperchase**, www.paperchase.co.uk

SECOND-HAND

Salvo: Useful directory service linking various dealers of architectural and reclaimed salvage with customers, as well as listing classified ads for the sale of low-value antique, reclaimed, and salvaged items.
USA/UK: www.salvo.web

The Salvation Army: Selling a selection of donated goods through their network of family stores (USA) and charity shops (UK), all profits go straight back into their charitable organization.
USA: www.salvationarmyusa.org/800-728-7825
UK: www.salvationarmy.co.uk/020 7367 4500

Emmaus: Known for their wide selection of vintage and retro furniture and homewares, this charity organization has various branches throughout the UK.
UK: www.emmaus.org.uk/01223 576103

eBay: If you're looking for a particular item, let eBay do the hard work for you: while logged in, click on the "advanced" option, adjust your search criteria to suit your requirements, then save that search. You can then opt for eBay to send you a daily tailored email with items matching your description.
USA: www.ebay.com
UK: www.ebay.co.uk

Listing websites

Find out where local flea markets and car boot fairs are happening in your area via listing sites. Don't forget to check local newspapers too, for smaller events like yard sales or jumble sales.
USA: **Flea Markets Across America**
www.fleamarketsacrossamerica.com
UK: **Car Boot Junction**
www.carbootjunction.com

BEST FOR BARGAINS

HomeGoods/HomeSense: The homes division of TK Maxx, this interiors-focused brand (known as HomeGoods in the USA and HomeSense in the UK) offers an ever-changing selection of previous-season homewares from a mixture of brands, at greatly reduced prices.
USA: www.homegoods.com/800-888-0776
UK: www.homesense.com/01923 473561

Members-only discount shopping
Sign up or log in to these sites to save large amounts off RRPs.
USA: **Fab**, www.fab.com/877-463-4322
UK: **Fab**, www.eu.fab.com/0800 7645 3546
USA: **Gilt**, www.gilt.com/877-280-0545
UK: **Achica**, www.achica.com

Fun and affordable
Add a touch of fun with some quirky, cheap accessories.
USA: **Delphinium Home**
www.delphiniumhome.com/212-333-7732
UK: **Tiger**, www.tigerstores.co.uk

Well priced, on-trend furniture can be worth the investment and help break up an all-vintage look.
USA: **Blu Dot**
www.bludot.com/612-782-1844
UK: **Alexander and Pearl**
www.alexanderandpearl.co.uk/020 8508 0411
UK: **Loaf**, www.loaf.com/0845 468 0698

Bemz: Ingenius Swedish company specializing in creating removable slip covers for many standard pieces of IKEA furniture, allowing you to create a whole new look for far less than buying new.
USA: www.bemz.com/+46-8-664-6200
UK: www.bemz.com/0800 048 8404

FREE STUFF

Freecycle: Allows users to offer up unwanted household items, free of charge, on the proviso that you collect it yourself within the agreed timeframe.
USA: www.freecycle.org
UK: www.uk.freecycle.org

Craig's List: Listing everything from jobs to gig tickets, this American-founded site now has a UK version, too. To find household freebies, click on your nearest city/town/area, then select the "free stuff" section under the For Sale category.
USA/UK: www.craigslist.org

Gumtree: The number one listings site for free classified ads in the UK; select its "Freebies" category within search listings to find items being given away.
UK: www.gumtree.com

PAINT & DIY

Annie Sloan Chalk Paint: A unique paint developed by Sloan, its tough, textural consistency means it can be applied to a multitude of difficult surfaces, such as melamine and metal furniture, plant pots and even fabric, without the need for primer.
USA: www.anniesloan.com/504-305-5531
UK: www.anniesloan.com/01865 247296

Plastikote: A wide range of spraypaints suitable for a multitude of different finishes and functions, and with a great selection of colors available.
USA www.plastikote.com/866-222-8714
UK www.plastikote.com/01223 836400

3M Command: The renters' best friend, this clever company offers a range of removable sticky strips and hooks from which to hang myriad items or create a gallery wall, all without damaging the wall surface.
USA: www.command.com/800-934-7355
UK: www.3mdirect.co.uk/0845 604 3697

Decorate Now: Useful for city dwellers without cars, this website stocks paints and DIY products from a number of different brands, and will deliver to your door.
UK: www.decoratenow.com/01323 436180

Paint-mixing services
The perfect choice when you have a specific color in mind; look for brands that offer different base paints suitable for surfaces other than walls, such as woodwork, metal, and exterior surfaces.

Valspar: With its precision paint color-matching service, Valspar can "read" (and recreate) any color the human eye can see.
USA: www.valsparpaint.com/800-845-9061
UK: www.valsparpaint.co.uk/0844 736 9174

Dulux: Its TailorMade system of over 1,200 colors is divided into "mood" palettes, to help ensure that the hues you pick will also create the effect you are after.
UK: www.dulux.co.uk/08444 817817

Sherwin Williams: As well as over 1,500 paint colors, it has its Faux Impressions collections for an unusual range of finishes.
USA: www.sherwin-williams.com/800-474-3794

Wood-cutting services:
If you want to get wood cut to size for shelving or DIY projects and don't have the tools to do it yourself, visit a DIY store that offers a cutting service for free (or a small fee) if you buy the wood from them first.
USA: **Home Depot**
www.homedepot.com/800-466-3337
UK: **B&Q**, www.diy.com/0845 609 6688

ART

Posters and prints

Poster Cabaret: Stocking over 2,500 specially curated designs.
USA: www.postercabaret.com/512-614-0220 (worldwide shipping available)

Easy Art: thousands of art prints, frames and canvases, with most pieces coming in a choice of size and finishing options.
UK: www.easyart.com/0845 1662 732 (worldwide shipping available)

Platform sites

Bringing together a collective of artists and illustrators under one roof is a great way to discover new pieces, as well as supporting enterprise.
USA: **Brika**, www.brika.com
UK: **Outline Editions**
www.outline-editions.co.uk/020 8451 3400

Vintage style

Hatch Show Prints: A mixture of reprints of original advertising and music posters mixed with recent vintage-style designs, from Nashville, Tennessee.
USA: www.countrymusichalloffame.org (worldwide shipping available)

Wallography: vintage-style educational charts, beautifully recreated.
UK: www.wallography.co.uk/020 7924 1864

WALL COVERINGS

Removable wallpapers

Perfect for renters or homeowners reluctant to take such a bold decorating step, peel-and-stick removable wallpapers can add a little fun to a feature wall or a whole room.
US: **Tempaper Designs**
www.tempaperdesigns.com/732-920-2654
UK: **Photo Wall**, www.photowall.co.uk/020 3318 3660

Wall Stencils

Forget the clichéd stenciled borders of the 1990s: today, stencils come in an array of contemporary styles. Add a quirky detail in an unexpected corner, or go bold and create a repeat pattern over an entire wall.
USA: **Cutting Edge Stencils**
www.cuttingedgestencils.com
UK: **The Stencil Library**
www.stencil-library.co.uk/01661 844844

Patterned paint rollers

Create a wallpapered look in an instant that's easy to paint over when you need to get back to neutral.
USA: **Roller Wall**
www.rollerwall.com/301-838-0450
UK: **The Painted House**
www.the-painted-house.co.uk

Wall murals

From a stick-on poster to a full-scale super-sized wall design, nothing creates a talking point quite like a giant photograph or design. Opt for the "Just Stick it Up" finish to keep it removable.
USA/UK: **Surface View** (see their Slim Aarons mural on page 98)
www.surfaceview.co.uk/+44 (0)118 922 1327 (worldwide shipping available)

Wall stickers

A great way to add a splash of design to walls, doors, and even furniture.

Blik: huge range of designs, from retro video game motifs to independent illustrators.
USA: www.whatisblik.com/866-262-2545

Lou Rota: bijou range of quirky bug stickers, as seen on page175
UK: www.lourota.com

All Posters: huge range of over 40,000 decal designs.
UK: www.allposters.co.uk/020 8435 6555

Tile stickers

Temporarily transform tired tiles in your kitchen or bathroom.

Mibo: removable "tile tattoos" in some great retro designs.
USA: www.2Jane.com/888-667-6961
UK: www.mibo.co.uk/01273 208888

Stick and Go: If you prefer a more natural look, try out these vinyl stickers that mimic authentic tile styles and can be stuck on and cut to fit with scissors.
USA: www.stickandgo.com/01144 1299 851001
UK: www.stickandgo.com/01299 851001

Wallpaper

If you're not able to hang wallpaper the usual way, think of it as artwork instead and experiment with using a roll on a wooden panel or covering a canvas.

Cole & Son: A classic British brand showcasing a fantastic range of unusual wallpaper designs as well as borders and murals, such as the pen design mural shown on page 84.
UK: www.cole-and-son.com/020 8442 8844

Flavor Paper: a rock-and-roll range of fun and funky designs.
USA: www.flavorpaper.com/718-422-0230

Wallpaper Direct: huge range of wallpaper brands stocked under one virtual roof, with something for any pricepoint and style. As well as classic designs, look for unusual wood effect and *trompe l'oeil* patterns.
USA: www.wallpaperdirect.com/855-823-9754
UK: www.wallpaperdirect.com/01323 430886

CRAFT SUPPLIES

Craft superstores

While online shopping is fantastic for convenience, browsing the aisles of a bricks-and-mortar store can help you discover new crafts.

USA: Jo-Ann
www.joann.com/1-888-739-4120
UK: Hobbycraft
www.hobbycraft.co.uk/0845 051 6599
UK: Fred Aldous
www.fredaldous.co.uk/0161 236 4224

Discounted designer fabrics
USA: Warehouse Fabrics Inc
www.warehousefabricsinc.com/205-487-8040
UK: Curtain Factory Outlet
www.curtainfactoryoutlet.co.uk/020 8492 0093

Colorful oilcloth and PVC fabrics
USA: Oilcloth by the Yard
www.oilclothbytheyard.com/610-888-2037
USA: Mexican Sugar Skull
www.mexicansugarskull.com/707-537-9787
UK: Viva la Frida, www.vivalafrida.co.uk

DIY window treatments
Making your own curtains and shades (or blinds) can not only be much cheaper than buying ready-made from the shops, but also offers the chance to choose from a far wider array of fabrics. If you already have a fabric you want to use, all you will need to buy is the necessary tapes or kits to make it up.
USA: Drapery Sewing Supplies
www.draperysewingsupplies.com/877-874-2202
UK: Colly Brook Fine Furnishings
www.collybrook.co.uk/01584 781255

Washi tape
Decorative Japanese masking tape that can be used to add (removable) color and pattern to many surfaces in the home, from walls and tiles to furniture and accessories. Look out for the ingenious MT Casa line of extra-wide tapes specifically designed for interiors.
USA/UK: Modes, www.modes4u.com
USA: Wishy Washy, www.wishywashi.com
UK: Lovely Tape, www.lovelytape.co.uk

PLANTS AND GARDENS

Royal Horticultural Society: For a novice gardener, the website of this classic British institution is packed with useful information.
USA/UK: www.rhs.org.uk

Sky planters
Boskke: When space is limited, sky planters can be a clever way to add greenery without cluttering surfaces.
USA/UK: www.boskke.com

Glass terrariums
Style your own plant vignettes and add doll's house accessories for a quirky look. If space is tight, try a hanging variety.
USA: Save on Crafts
www.save-on-crafts.com/831-768-8428
UK: Chive, www.chiveuk.com

Air plants
Requiring just water and light (no need for green fingers), it's easy to look after one of these unusual beauties.
USA: Air Plant City
www.airplantcity.com/321-453-6054
UK: Just Air Plants
www.justairplants.com/0118 324 3949

Gardening accessories
Jazz up your garden with interesting pots and décor.
USA: Terrain
www.shopterrain.com/877-583-7724
UK: Garden Beet
www.gardenbeet.com/020 3397 2337

INSPIRATIONAL WEBSITES

IKEA Hackers: teaming with brilliant ideas ("hacks"), this unofficial, fan-run website features thousands of reader-submitted DIY projects for modifying or repurposing IKEA pieces.
www.ikeahackers.net

Design*Sponge: This super-site, run by writer Grace Bonney and her dedicated team in Brooklyn, New York, is understandably sympathetic to the needs of renters and small-space dwellers. Their "sneak peek" house tours allow you to specify if you'd like to see rented or owned homes.
www.designsponge.com

Nothing But the Rent: Set up by a London-based homeowner-turned-renter, to share her renter-friendly home decorating discoveries with others.
www.nothingbuttherent.co.uk

Junkaholique: Charming blog by jewelry designer and vintage-lover Artemis Russell, chronicling her flea-market adventures and tales of decorating her rented apartments and, latterly, her first home.
www.junkaholique.com

Pinterest: Now one of the most powerful (and much-loved) social-media sites, this invaluable resource allows you to search through thousands of images "pinned" by its users, via keyword searches. Set up your own boards to group ideas and inspiration in one place.
www.pinterest.com
Check out the Pinterest page set up for this book—full of home-for-now-friendly ideas scoured from across the web, as well as links to book reviews and mentions.
www.pinterest.com/joannathornhill/homefornowbook

Joanna Thornhill—to find out more about me, see examples of work from my portfolio, keep up to date with book news, and link through to my other social-media networks, log on!
www.joannathornhill.co.uk

INDEX

CONTRIBUTOR INFORMATION AND ADDITIONAL CREDITS

Key: l = left, r = right, t = top, b = bottom, c = center, Pr = project made and designed by the respective homeowner/tenant

Anna Alicia
Jewelry and homeware designer, London, UK; lives in a shared-ownership apartment with her husband
www.aalicia.bigcartel.com
Pages 8l, 12, 49, 64–65, 76r, 174r

Becky Nolan and Barny Read
Vintage shop owners, London, UK; rent a one-bedroom converted Victorian apartment
www.thepeanutvendor.co.uk
Pages 4t, 8r, 18, 48, 56r, 74l, 79r, 85r, 87, 108r, 128, 134, 145l

Carole Poirot
Lifestyle blogger and interiors stylist, London, UK; rents a three-bedroom apartment with her partner and teenage son
www.mademoisellepoirot.com
Pages 4b, 31l, 37r (Erykah Badu portrait by Carole Poirot), 42tl, 51b, 68 (Moroccan Man painting by Carole Poirot), 69, 78l, 119tr, 121, 124l, 141r, 147Pr, 152b

Clare Nicolson
Textile designer and interiors stylist, London, UK; rents a small studio apartment
www.clarenicolson.com
Pages 9, 39r, 56l, 60, 80, 82l, 110b, 132, 148, 152tl, 165t, 171Pr, 188

Dion Salvador Lloyd
Artist, Brighton, UK; first-time owner, living in a two-bedroom apartment
www.dionsalvador.co.uk
Pages 15, 33r, 40–41, 42b, 79l, 84, 96, 109, 119tl, 122r (painting by Dion Salvador Lloyd), 130, 164, 187

Hannah Ricci and Gavin Kettle
Furniture makers and restorers (both), florist and interiors writer (Hannah), Staffordshire, UK; rent a two-bedroom apartment
www.rubyrhino.co.uk
Pages 1, 29l, 32, 55, 78br (Poolside by Slim Aarons wall mural courtesy of Surface View—also seen on page 98), 98, 116r, 123r, 125-127Pr, 131, 133, 144, 172, 189

Holly Wales and Stephen Smith
Illustrators, London, UK; rent an open-plan studio space
www.hollywales.com/www.neasdencontrolcentre.com
Pages 7, 62–63, 112 (artwork by Stephen Smith), 113, 145r

Jane Petrie
Costume designer, London, UK; first-time owner, living in a two-bedroom ex-council apartment with her husband and young son
www.costumedetail.blogspot.co.uk
Pages 28, 50, 72, 94,103 (project made and designed by Rocky Alvarez for Jane Petrie, with instructions adapted by author), 135, 142, 154, 174l

Karin Lindroos
Interiors stylist, writer, and photographer, Finland; rents a one-bedroom apartment in Helsinki with her husband and young daughter, and has access to a one-bedroom seaside apartment in Tammisarri (both are seen in this book)
www.karin.ratata.fi
Pages 11, 29r, 38tl, 74r, 77l, 82r, 90, 106, 110t, 119b, 122l, 137, 141l, 168, 177, 183r

Kimberly Hughes
Interiors blogger, Manchester, UK; owns a three-bedroom house with her partner
www.swoonworthy.co.uk
Pages 16, 20, 30Pr, 59Pr, 76l, 99, 100, 118, 123l, 124r, 162, 169r, 180, 183r

Maria Meder
Interiors blogger, Järvenpää, Finland; first-time owner, living in a two-bedroom house with her partner and teenage son
www.diagnoosisisustusmania.blogspot.co.uk
Pages 2, 3, 21, 39l, 42tr, 46, 54t, 54bl, 75, 77r, 108l, 111, 114, 143, 161, 167

Ninette Bahne
Housewife and blogger, Pargas, Finland; owns a four-bedroom house with her husband and three children
www.familjenbahne.com
Pages 23–25Pr, 26, 31r, 34, 35l, 36, 52, 53, 71, 78tr, 83, 86, 89Pr, 92, 115, 119tc, 150–151, 152tc, 152tr, 153, 159Pr, 179, 182, 183l, 184–185

Philippa Stanton
Artist, Brighton, UK; owner, living with her teenage son
www.philippastanton.com
Pages 14, 33l, 38tc, 38tr, 51tl, 51tr, 95, 120, 155, 156-157, 165b, 178

Saija Starr
Visual artist, Helsinki, Finland; rents a one-bedroom apartment with her boyfriend
www.cosyhomeblogi.wordpress.com
Pages 22, 38bl, 54r, 85l, 93, 101, 105, 116l, 138, 140, 166, 169l

Tom Chalet
London, UK; first-time owner, living in a new-build, one-bedroom apartment
www.tomchalet.co.uk
Pages 19, 37l, 66–67, 81, 117, 175, 176

ACKNOWLEDGMENTS

Firstly, a big thanks to the team at CICO for the enormous amount of trust they have placed in me and my little idea, and for helping turn that idea into a fully-fledged, proper book. Special thanks to Cindy Richards, Sally Powell, and especially Carmel Edmonds for their tireless work and guidance, and to editor Alison Bolus, designer Vicky Rankin, and illustrator Harriet de Winton for turning my words and images into these beautiful pages and projects.

To my wonderful photographers, Emma Mitchell and James Gardiner, for their patience and skill in creating such marvellous imagery that really capture the spirit of what this book is about. Additional thanks to Clare Nicolson, for her styling assistance and support on our mega four-locations-in-two-days London leg, and to Rita Platts, for her invaluable photographic assistance and charming company during our week shooting in Finland.

This book would quite simply not exist without the amazing renters and home-for-now owners who so generously opened their doors and let us photograph their wonderful spaces. Each and every one of them blew me away with their creativity and ingenuity (as well as leaving me with a serious case of house envy!). I do hope this feeling translates through the book and that readers will feel just as inspired as I did when looking at all they have achieved. So here's to Anna, Barny and Becky, Carole, Clare, Dion, Hannah and Gavin, Holly and Steve, Jane, Karin, Kimberly, Philippa, Saija, and Tom, plus an extra-special thank-you to Ninette and Maria for so kindly introducing us to their local cuisine during our visits! Thanks also to everyone who took the time to help me on my house hunting quest by nominating themselves, or suggesting others, to feature in this book (especially Emily Blunden, Jenny Voyce, Charlotte Love, and Charlene Mullen, whose suggestions directly led me to several of my featured contributors).

Finally, personal thanks to my parents—firstly for raising me to craft, sew, make, and DIY (I never expected to need these skills in my professional life so I'm glad I paid attention!) and for their "consultancy" on the numerous DIY and craft queries that arose while writing this book. A special mention to my niece, Natasha, for her enthusiastic support, along with my various friends and colleagues who have kept me going throughout this process. And last, but by no means least, an extra-special thank you to my amazing partner, Paul, for his unfaltering love, support, and faith that I could do this, and for doing the washing up for the best part of a year while I did. This book is for you.